KALI LINUX

The ultimate guide to learn, execute linux programming and Hacking tools for computers

[Steve Eddison]

Table of Contents

Book Description

In today's world, <u>computers </u>are essential to most people's everyday life. We use computers all the time: for work, to communicate, or even to relax by watching our favorite movies and TV shows or playing our favorite games. Computers are also always in the background, working to make our lives easier: computers and complex software help run our traffic lights, the air traffic control systems at airports, and even control the inventory and tracking system of various businesses. Even modern cars have computers built into them, integrated into the ECU, or electronic control unit. Suffice it to say, modern life as we know it is almost entirely dependent on computers working and working in the proper way.

As computers control a lot of things, even sensitive and important information such as data storage for businesses, identities, and bank details, there are a lot of unscrupulous people out there who want to be able to take advantage of the world's dependency on computers. There are people who want to take advantage of certain vulnerabilities in the various computer systems around the world, often for nefarious purposes, such as stealing money, information, or even sometimes simply disabling the computer system in question. This exploitation is known as "hacking".

"Hacking" is made possible by the interconnected nature of computer networks. This is why some companies and businesses choose to improve security by having isolated servers, connected only to internal networks, which stop outside users from gaining unauthorized access. However, it is not possible for all computer networks to be private networks, and there are networks that have to be accessible by computers outside the network, meaning that there have to be additional defenses put in place, as this connection with outside computers may serve as an angle of attack for a hacker.

Introduction

Congratulations on purchasing *Kali Linux* and thank you for doing so.

In layman's terms, hacking is the act of breaking into someone else's computer to which you have no access and stealing private information by circumventing the security measures. It is dangerous because it sabotages the entire computer system.

The origin of the word "hacking" can be traced back to the 1960's and 1970's. Some hackers, called Yippe, were anti-war protestors and members of the Youth International Party. They played pranks in the streets, and most of their prank techniques were taught within their group. It is important to note that they were involved in tapping telephone lines as well.

Gradually, what was called a prank grew to another level and became known as hacking. However, this time their tools were state-of-the-art mega core processors and multi-function plasma screens.

Hacking tactics are increasingly being used by terrorist organizations for numerous acts of evil, including obtaining illegal funding, spreading propaganda, launching missiles, threatening the government and gathering intelligence about secret military movements.

In this book, various types of hacking will be broken down and explained. Step by step instructions will be provided so that you can protect yourself from hackers in your office and home, as well as on the internet.

Chapter 1) What is Kali Linux?

Kali is a flavor of Linux distributions that is Debian-based and was created specifically for its application in the security domain, which focused primarily on Security Auditing and Penetration Testing. Kali comes equipped with hundreds of tools that are aimed at various tasks used for information security. These include Security Research, Penetration Testing, Reverse Engineering, Computer Forensics, etc. Offensive Security, a company that is a world leader in information security training, is the company that developed Kali Linux and now funds its maintenance.

Kali Linux is a successor of BackTrack Linux. BackTrack Linux was a Linux distribution which was developed for security tasks and was aimed at penetration testing and digital forensics. After the deprecation of BackTrack Linux in 2013, Kali Linux was released in March 2013 as a complete reboot of BackTrack Linux from top to bottom in compliance with all the Debian development standards.

Let's go through the features of Kali Linux in brief before we deep dive into this book.

Features of Kali Linux

Penetration testing tools

Kali Linux comes with more than 600 tools for penetration testing. If one were to go through the number of tools available in the predecessor that is BackTrack, there were a lot of tools which were not functional or were just duplicates of functions that were already available in other tools. These have been eliminated from the Kali Linux releases.

Free to use

BackTrack Linux was completely free of cost to use, and this has been continued with Kali Linux as well. As a Kali Linux user, you will never have to pay for the operating system or the tools it comes equipped with.

Open Source

Kali Linus is committed to the model of Open Source, and therefore the Kali Linux development tree is available to everyone on the Internet. The source code for Kali Linux is available on gitlab and is available to anyone who wants to make customizations to it and rebuild the packages to suit their specific needs.

Compliance with FHS

Kali complies with the Filesystem Hierarchy Standard, which is followed by all Linux flavors. This will make it easy for the system to locate binaries, libraries, support files, etc.

Support for wireless devices

One of the concerns with Linux systems in the past has been its support for wireless devices. Kali Linux has been developed and built in such a way that it will support a wide range of wireless devices, and it will be compatible with the hardware of a vast variety and therefore will support USB and most wireless devices.

Custom kernel

Kali Linux kernel comes equipped with the latest injection patches. As penetration testers, this helps the development team to conduct wireless assessments with ease.

They are developed in a secure environment. The development team of Kali Linux includes a very small group of individuals, and they are trusted to make commits to the repositories and packages for Kali Linux, all of which is achieved using secure protocols via multiple channels.

GPG signed

Every developer who has worked on packages for Kali Linux signs it and subsequently, the repositories sign the package as well.

Language support

Penetration tools are usually written in English. However, Kali Linux developers have ensured that Kali includes language support for users from around the world so that more users can work in their native language and find tools on Kali that they can use to complete their tasks.

Customizable

Kali developers understand enough to know that not all users can accept their interface design. Therefore, they have made it very easy for the adventurous users to customize the system as per their requirement right from the top till the kernel.

Support for ARMEL and ARMHF: ARM-based single-board devices such as the BeagleBone Black and Raspberry Pi are popular among the users, mainly because they are so inexpensive. Therefore, Kali Linux has been built in a way such that it is as robust as possible and has a fully functional installation that will support both ARMHF and ARMEL systems. A wide range of ARM devices are supported by Kali Linux and tools for ARM are kept up to date and at par with the rest of the distributions.

What's Different about Kali Linux?

Kali Linux is developed specifically to meet the needs of professionals who are looking for tools related to security auditing and penetration testing. There are several tools integrated with Kali Linux, which help meet these needs.

Single user - Root

Linux operating system usually practices operating systems that have a root user and other users with fewer privileges than the root user. Kali Linux, however, practices a single user concept that is the root with all access. This has been done because most of the tools that are required for penetration testing using Kali required high access. Thus, although most Linux flavors practice the policy to enable root access only when essential, Kali Linux use cases use the approach of using root user to decrease the burden of additional users.

Network services disabled

By default, network services are disabled on Kali Linux. Kali uses a system service that disables all network services. This helps in the installation of various applications on Kali Linux in a secure environment irrespective of the packages that are installed. Bluetooth is also blacklisted by default.

Customized kernel

Kali Linux comes equipped with a kernel that is completely customized and patched for wireless injection.

Minimal repositories

Kali Linux has minimal and trusted repositories only. Given the motive with which Kali Linux was developed, it makes absolute sense to maintain the integrity of the system. Therefore, third-party applications for Kali are kept at a bare minimum to achieve the goal of security. While many users are tempted to add third-party repositories to their sources and lists, doing so increases the risk of breaking your Kali installation.

Is Kali Linux Right For You?

Given that we are authoring a book about Kali Linux, one might expect that we recommend it to everyone in our client base to use Kali Linux. Kali Linux, however, is developed specifically for testers who are into penetration testing and those who are security specialists. Therefore, if you are just beginning to start as a Linus user, is NOT recommended at all as a system which you are looking to use as a general desktop operating system for your day to day activities such as gaming, development, web design, etc.

Kali Linux can pose as a challenge even for veteran users in the Linux domain. Kali, unlike other open source Linux projects, is not a wide-open source project, mainly because of security concerns. The development team consists of a very small number of users, and the packages that are developed for Kali Linux and committed to repositories are signed by the individual developer first and then by the entire team. Also, the upstream or third-party repository from which the packages are updated, or new packages are pulled is very small. Adding software from repositories to your Kali operating system from third party sources that are not tested and verified by the Kali Linux team can cause harm to your system.

While the architecture of Kali Linux is highly customizable, adding random and unrelated packages that do not fit in the Kali Linux domain and are not downloaded from the regular sources will not work on Kali. Kali Linux will not support commands such as apt-add-repository, PPAs, or LaunchPad. Also, if you are trying to install Steam on your Kali Linux OS, it will end up being a disaster. Installing mainstream packages like NodeJS on your Kali Linux system can also take a lot of research, time and patience. You should not begin working on the Kali Linux operating system:

- If you are just beginning to work with a Linux operating system, without having used a Linux system ever before in life

- If you do not have the basic knowledge or competence to administer a system, if you are just looking for your first Linux system to start learning Linux

- If you are just looking for an operating system to do your daily activities, Kali Linux is not the operating system that you may want to begin with

Over and above, the misuse of penetration testing tools and security within a computer network, without any authorization, may result in irreversible damage and the consequences of such damage may get you into personal or legal trouble. The excuse that "You did not know what you were doing" will not work in such cases.

In contrast, if you are aiming at becoming a professional in penetration testing with the sole goal of becoming a certified professional, there is no better operating system that you can find than Kali Linux, at any price and especially for free.

So, to summarize and answer the question we asked when we started this chapter, if you are looking to just start with the basics of Linux on Linux operating system, Kali Linux is not the deal for you. You should first begin with the simple versions of Linux such as Ubuntu, Debian, or Mint instead.

Chapter 2) Installing and downloading Kali Linux

Of course, the installation is necessary in order to use Kali Linux, and there are multiple ways we can install Kali Linux, from the most basic method: placing it on the system's hard disk drive; to more advanced methods, such as dual – booting Kali Linux with other operating systems. Let's get started!

Installing Kali Linux on your machine

Let's start with the most basic method of installation of the Kali Linux distribution: placing it on our system's hard disk drive. By now, the user should have already ensured that their system hardware is compatible (as a reminder, Kali Linux supports i386 / 32 – bit systems, amd64 / 64 – bit systems, and ARM / armel / armhf systems). The next step is ensuring that the system hardware, in addition to having compatible system architecture, should also meet the minimum hardware requirements, which are as follows:

Installing Kali Linux on your hard disk drive

Minimum of 20 gigabytes of free hard disk drive space for Kali Linux's installation
Minimum of 1 gigabyte of random access memory (RAM) for i386 and amd64 – based architecture (The more RAM the system has, the better the performance)
Native CD – DVD drive support, or USB boot support

Note as well that the i386 default images have PAE kernels enabled by default, so they can be run on systems that have above 4 gigabytes of RAM. Once the system hardware matches the Kali Linux compatibility and performance requirements, the ISO that was downloaded or rebuilt should be burned to a DVD, or a USB stick with the Kali Linux Live installation media should be readied. Note that in case there is no CD – DVD drive support, nor USB boot support, another option exists, being the Kali Linux Network Install, which will be discussed in a following section.

Installation Procedure

Once everything is ready, i.e all the requirements are met, and the Kali Linux software has been prepared and is ready to be installed, the first step would be to insert the installation media and boot it / run it (through the USB boot or the CD – DVD drive). Booting the medium should result in a window appearing with multiple options, such as "Live (amd64)", "Graphical Install", or simply "Install". The "graphical install" enables a GUI install, and the "install" initiates a text – mode installation process.

Once the installation method is selected, the window will then request the user to select their preferred system / software language, as well as place their country's location. In addition, a prompt may come out to request the user to configure their keyboard for the appropriate key – mapping. Once the language – country combination has been selected, and the keyboard properly mapped, the next step will be to input the geographical location of the user. Pressing "continue" after this step will instruct the installer to begin the process of installing the image by copying it to the hard disk drive, as well as probing the network interfaces of the device.

Once these steps are complete, the installer will request the user to input the host name of the system. The purpose of the host name is to identify the system to the network that it is connected to. The host name can be selected by the user and can be changed in the future. The next step is to choose a domain name, which forms part of the computer's address, found on the right side of the host name. This domain name is usually seen as the ".com", ".edu", ".net" suffixes. Note that this step is entirely optional, but if used, it would be prudent to ensure all the computers on the network share the same domain name to avoid errors or confusion.

Once the host and domain name have been selected, the system will then prompt the user to provide a name for the user account. Note that this account will NOT have root access and is meant to enable the system to have an account that can carry out non-administrative activities without admin – access for safety purposes. Upon providing a name, a user – ID will be created based on the given account name, but this ID can be edited to match the user's preference.

Once all the naming conventions have been set up, the system will check and configure the clock, by requesting for the time zone wherein the user is located. Note that this step still occurs even after having chosen the geographical location, and in fact it notes that in case the time zone the user is in is not listed, they can simply go back and choose the country they are currently located in.

After choosing the partition, the system installer will prompt the user one more time to check whether or not their chosen configuration is what they really want, allowing the user to double – check their configuration options, as installing the Kali Linux software makes numerous disk changes, and making an error in installation may cost a lot of time and effort to reverse and / or remedy. Once the configuration is confirmed, the installer will begin installation on the partitioned drive, and the result will be a near – complete installation. After this, the network mirrors can be configured by the user, and as Kali makes use of a central repository for the distribution of applications, it is necessary to set the network mirrors. Note that it may be possible that the installer will require the user to enter proxy information in case their network makes use of a proxy.

Once the network has been set up, one of the final steps is to install the "GRUB" boot loader in order to be able to boot Kali Linux. Note that in case there are no other operating systems currently installed, the user may choose to have GRUB as the master boot loader. In case of other operating systems, selecting GRUB as the master boot loader may render the other operating systems temporarily unbootable, but this may be fixed by manually changing the configuration later on in order to reset it. Once this is done, the user only has to reboot their system by clicking "continue", and this should reboot and load the newly – installed Kali Linux operating system.

Installing Kali Linux over a network (Preboot Execution Environment)

As earlier mentioned, the conventional method of installing Kali Linux requires either a USB boot capability or a CD – DVD drive that can be used for the installation media to be loaded on the system. A lot of the time, this method is used for business or enterprise Kali Linux deployments, where multiple devices need to have the Kali Linux distribution pre – loaded onto them in order for use. This pre – seeding can be done over the network, which is something useful especially when the devices have their USB and CD – DVD ports and drives disabled, as is common practice for business laptops and computers.

The first step in getting the Kali Linux distribution installed over a network, through a PXE (pre – boot execution environment), is to install the "**dnsmasq**", which provides the DCHP / TFTP server. Once the **dnsmasq** is installed, the next step would then be to edit the "**dnsmasq.conf**" file.

The previous code installs the **dnsmasq**. The following snippet of code will then allow the user to enable the boot – up of the DHCP, TFTP, and PXE, as well as allow the user to set the dhcp – range to match the environment. In addition, the gateway as well as the DNS servers can be re – defined using the dhcp – option directive as needed.

After all the necessary changes have been made, the **dnsmasq** must be restarted in order for these changes to properly take effect.

Once the **dnsmasq** has been restarted and the changes have taken effect, the next step is to make sure that the directory that will be holding the image of the Kali Linux netboot has been created, and that the proper image has been downloaded from the proper Kali Linux repositories.

That should create the requisite directory and initiate the needed download. The user can then simply boot the system that they intend to install Kali Linux on and configure it to boot from the connected network. The connected device should automatically retrieve an IP address from the PXE server and begin the Kali Linux installation process.

Installing Kali Linux as an encrypted disk install

Preliminary Requirements

Ensure that the device that they want to run Kali Linux on is properly protected, and in those cases, they may wish to create an installation that is encrypted with a secure password. By now, the user should have already ensured that their system hardware is compatible (as a reminder, Kali Linux supports i386 / 32 – bit systems, amd64 / 64 – bit systems, and ARM / armel / armhf systems). The next step is ensuring that the system hardware, in addition to having compatible system architecture, should also meet the minimum hardware requirements, which are as follows:

Minimum of 20 gigabytes of free hard disk drive space for Kali Linux's installation

Minimum of 1 gigabyte of random access memory (RAM) for i386 and amd64 – based architecture (The more RAM the system has, the better the performance)

Native CD – DVD drive support, or USB boot support

Note as well that the i386 default images have PAE kernels enabled by default, so they can be run on systems that have above 4 gigabytes of RAM. Once the system hardware matches the Kali Linux compatibility and performance requirements, the ISO that was downloaded or rebuilt should be burned to a DVD, or a USB stick with the Kali Linux Live installation media should be readied. Note that in case there is no CD – DVD drive support, nor USB boot support, another option exists, being the Kali Linux Network Install, which will be discussed in a following section.

Installation Procedure

Once everything is ready, i.e all the requirements are met, and the Kali Linux software has been prepared and is ready to be installed, the first step would be to insert the installation media and boot it / run it (through the USB boot or the CD – DVD drive). Booting the medium should result in a window appearing with multiple options, such as "Live (amd64)", "Graphical Install", or simply "Install". The "graphical install" enables a GUI install, and the "install" initiates a text – mode installation process.

Once the installation method is selected, the window will then request the user to select their preferred system / software language, as well as place their country's location. In addition, a prompt may come out to request the user to configure their keyboard for the appropriate key – mapping. Once the language – country combination has been selected, and the keyboard properly mapped, the next step will be to input the geographical location of the user. Pressing "continue" after this step will instruct the installer to begin the process of installing the image by copying it to the hard disk drive, as well as probing the network interfaces of the device.

Once these steps are complete, the installer will request the user to input the host name of the system. The purpose of the host name is to identify the system to the network that it is connected to. The host name can be selected by the user and can be changed in the future. The next step is to choose a domain name, which forms part of the computer's address, found on the right side of the host name. This domain name is usually seen as the ".com", ".edu", ".net" suffixes. Note that this step is entirely optional, but if used, it would be prudent to ensure all the computers on the network share the same domain name to avoid errors or confusion.

Once the host and domain name have been selected, the system will then prompt the user to provide a name for the user account. Note that this account will NOT have root access and is meant to enable the system to have an account that can carry out non-administrative activities without admin – access for safety purposes. Upon providing a name, a user – ID will be created based on the given account name, but this ID can be edited to match the user's preference.

Once all the naming conventions have been set up, the system will check and configure the clock, by requesting for the time zone wherein the user is located. Note that this step still occurs even after having chosen the geographical location, and in fact it notes that in case the time zone the user is in is not listed, they can simply go back and choose the country they are currently located in.

After choosing the partition, the system installer will prompt the user one more time to check whether or not their chosen configuration is what they really want, allowing the user to double – check their configuration options, as installing the Kali Linux software makes numerous disk changes, and making an error in installation may cost a lot of time and effort to reverse and / or remedy. After the confirmation, the Kali Linux installer will require the user to set a password, which will be required every time that the Kali Linux instance is booted up. Once the password is verified, the user can simply click "continue".

Once the configuration is confirmed and the password selected, the installer will begin on the partitioned drive, and the result will be a near – complete installation. After this, the network mirrors can be configured by the user, and as Kali makes use of a central repository for the distribution of applications, it is necessary to set the network mirrors. Note that it may be possible that the installer will require the user to enter proxy information in case their network makes use of a proxy.

Once the network has been set up, one of the final steps is to install the "GRUB" boot loader in order to be able to boot Kali Linux. Note that in case there are no other operating systems currently installed, the user may choose to have GRUB as the master boot loader. In case of other operating systems, selecting GRUB as the master boot loader may render the other operating systems temporarily unbootable, but this may be fixed by manually changing the configuration later on in order to reset it. Once this is done, the user only has to reboot their system by clicking "continue", and this should reboot and load the newly – installed Kali Linux operating system.

Dual Booting Kali Linux and the Windows Operating System

Some users may have a need of having two operating systems on one device – for example, budget constraints may mean that they can only really afford to have one device, so they need their laptop to be able to multi – task, or perhaps the user simply prefers to have the option of using Kali Linux on their Windows – loaded device. Whatever the reason, Kali Linux can be dual – booted alongside the Windows operating system.

For the purposes of this particular tutorial, we will be assuming that the Windows operating system will be taking up the full capacity of the hard disk drive's space, and as such, we will teach the reader how to partition the hard disk drive in order to lessen the dedicated size for Windows, enough that the user will be able to boot Kali Linux.

Much like any other Kali Linux installation, the user has to ensure that the system hardware, in addition to having compatible system architecture, should also meet the minimum hardware requirements, which are as follows:

Minimum of 20 gigabytes of free hard disk drive space for Kali Linux's installation (after re – partition) Native CD – DVD drive support, or USB boot support Note that the creation of a dual – boot is not possible using the PXE system, meaning that native CD – DVD drive support or USB boot support is indispensable when creating the dual – boot setup.

Creating a Partition

In order to create a partition, the installation media should be booted – this means loading the downloaded Kali Linux ISO or booting the Kali Linux Live, whichever is applicable. Booting the medium should result in a window appearing with multiple options, such as "Live (amd64)", "Graphical Install", or simply "Install". The "graphical install" enables a GUI install, and the "install" initiates a text – mode installation process. Once this is loaded and the menu has opened, the "Live" option should be selected. This "Live" option will boot up the Kali Linux desktop and allow the user to access some of the applications and tools.

The tool that we are looking for here is the **gparted** program. The user should look for and launch the **gparted** program. **Gparted** will be the application that we will use in order to re – size and shrink the Windows partition in order to let us install the Kali Linux distribution.

Once the **gparted** program has launched, there will be options available to the user. There will be a list of partitions, and the user has to select the partition that has Windows loaded on it. Where it is situated on the list will depend on the user's configuration, but most configurations have it as the second and larger – sized hard disk drive partition. Once the partition containing the Windows boot is selected, simply right – click the partition and select "resize / move" in order to resize the partition in question. Resize it in such a way that there will be at least twenty gigabytes (20 GB) in the "unallocated" portion, as this will be used for the Kali Linux installation further on.

Upon resizing, there should be a button on the application dashboard shaped like a green check – mark, which is an "Apply All Operations" button. Simply click this in order to finalize the partition. Once the partition has been finalized, simply exit the **gparted** application and reboot the system. This should re – size the hard disk drive and free up enough space for the user to install a fresh version of Kali Linux.

Installation Procedure

Once the hard disk has already been properly partitioned, simply run / boot the installation media once again and select the install option. Follow the same steps as provided in the section of "Installing Kali Linux on your hard drive" with one key difference, notably the selection of the partition option, which will be shown in the next paragraph.

Upon completion of the preliminary steps, i.e language, location, time zone, and keyboard mapping, the installer will now probe the system's disks and offer five possible choices for installation. These choices are: guided – use the largest continuous free space (note that this is a non – default option that only shows up once a partition is created using the **gparted** application). Upon selection (in this case, "guided – use the largest continuous free space" option should be used), the system installer will now install the Kali Linux distribution on the previously "unallocated" space that we previously freed up by making use of the **gparted** application. The system installer will give the user the option to have "all files in one partitioned" as the default recommended option, but also allows for a separate / home partition as well as a separate / home, / usr, / var, and / tmp partition setup.

How to work with Kali Linux

Before a hacker can hack into a system, he or she must complete certain processes. Some of these are:

1. RECONNAISSANCE

To avoid being hacked, you should keep your private information very secure. The word "reconnaissance" in this context is a means by which the hacker tries to gather all information regarding you (the target) and any weak spots in your system. The hacker uses this step to find as much information as possible about the target.

2. SCANNING AND ENUMERATION

Scanning involves the use of intelligent system port scanning to examine your system's open ports and vulnerable spots. The attacker can use numerous automated tools to check and test your system's vulnerabilities.

3. GAINING ACCESS

If the hacker was able to complete the two phases above, his/her next stage is to gain access to your system. This stage is where all of the hacker's fun will begin. He or she will use the weaknesses discovered during the reconnaissance and scanning of your system to break into your connection. The hacker could exploit your local area network, your internet (both online or offline) or your local access to a PC. In the real sense, the moment a hacker breaks into your system or network, the hacker is considered to be the owner of that system. The security breach refers to the stage in which the hacker can use evil techniques to damage your system.

4. MAINTAINING ACCESS

In the previous phase, we said that once a black hat hacker hacks your system, it is no longer yours. In this phase, after the hacker has breached your security access and hacked your system completely, he or she can gain future access to your computer by creating a backdoor. So even if you get access to that computer system or network again, you still can't be sure you are in total control. The hacker could install some scripts that would allow access to your system even when you think the threat is gone.

5. CLEARING TRACKS

The hacker gained access to your system and at the same time maintained access to that system. What do you think the hacker will do next? The hacker will then clear all of his or her tracks to avoid detection by security personnel or agencies so that he or she can continue using the system. In other cases, the hacker may do this just to prevent legal action against him or her. Today, many security breaches go undetected. There have been cases in which firewalls were circumvented even when vigilant log checking was in place.

By now, you should have some insight into what hacking is all about. Now we will outline the fundamental security guidelines that will protect you, your system and your information from external threats. All of the information we will provide is based on practical methodologies that have been used successfully. These methodologies will help prevent a computer system from being attacked and ravaged by malicious users.

Update Your OS (Operating System)

Operating systems are open to different types of attacks. On a daily basis, new viruses are released; this alone should make you cautious because your operating system might be vulnerable to a new set of threats. This is why the vendors of these operating systems release new updates on a regular basis, so that they can stay ahead of new threats. his will help you improve your security and reduce the risk of your system becoming a host to viruses.

Update Your Software

In the previous section, we talked about the importance of an update. Updated software is equipped with more efficiency and convenience, and even has better built-in security features. Thus, it is imperative that you frequently update your applications, browsers and other programs.

Antivirus

Based on our research, we have seen that some operating systems are open to a lot of attacks, especially Microsoft or Windows platforms. One way you can protect your system from viruses is through an antivirus program. An antivirus program can save you in many ways. There are many antivirus programs (free or paid) that you can install on your system to protect against threats. A malicious hacker can plant a virus on your system through the internet, but with a good antivirus scan, you can see the threat and eliminate it. As with any other software or program, your antivirus software needs frequent updates to be 100 percent effective.

Anti-Spyware

This program is also important, as you don't want trojan programs on your system. You can get many anti-spyware programs on the internet; just make sure you go for one that has received good ratings.

Go for Macintosh

The Windows operating system is very popular and therefore many hackers and crackers target it. You may have read articles and blogs saying that Macintosh operating systems are less secure; however, Macintosh is immune to many threats that affect Windows. Thus, we urge you to try the Macintosh platform.

Avoid Shady Sites

When you are browsing Facebook, you may come across unknown people who send you messages with links, some in the form of clickbait. Avoid clicking on such links. Also, you must avoid porn sites, or sites that promise you things that are too good to be true. Some of these sites promise you free music when you click on a link, while others offer free money or a movie. These sites are run by malicious hackers who are looking for ways to harm your computer with their malware links. Take note that on some malicious sites, you don't even have to click on anything to be hacked. A good browser will always inform you of a bad site before it takes you there. Always listen to your browser's warnings and head back to safety if necessary.

Firewall

If you are a computer specialist working in an organization, you might come across cases in which more than one computer system's OS is under one network. In situations like these, you must install software that provides a security firewall. The Windows operating system has an inbuilt firewall that you can activate and use directly. This firewall feature comes in different versions of Windows, including Windows XP, Windows Professional, Windows 10 and the other versions.

Spam

You can be hacked from spamming too. Email providers have taken the initiative to classify emails according to a set of parameters. Some emails will be sent directly into the inbox and some will be sent to the spam folder. To be safe, avoid opening emails that look suspicious. Some of them will have attachments that you should not open. Regardless of the security measures taken by email providers, some spam emails will still pass their filters and come straight into your inbox. Avoid opening such emails and do not download the attachments that come with them.

Back-Up Options

Some files will contain confidential information, such as personal files, financial data and work-related documents you cannot afford to lose. You should register with Google Drive, Onedrive and other cloud drive companies so that you can upload your files as a form of backup. You can also purchase an external hard disk and transfer all of your important files to it. Take all these security measures because a single malicious software can scramble your data regardless of the antivirus you have installed. You can't reverse some actions once they've been taken, so always have a backup.

Password

This is the most important aspect of security. The importance of a strong password can never be overstated. Starting from your e-mail, your documents or even a secure server, a good password is the first and last line of defense against external threats. There are two categories of passwords: weak and strong. A weak password is made by using your mobile phone number, your name, a family member's name or something that can be guessed easily. Avoid using this kind of password, as even an amateur hacker can guess it.

Some people use dates such as their birthday or a special anniversary; however, that is still not safe. When creating a password, take your time and do some basic math because your password must contain both letters and numbers. You can even combine it with special characters. For instance, if your initial password is "jack," you can make it "J@ck007." A password like this will be almost impossible to guess even though it's simple. Furthermore, avoid writing down your passwords. Your password isn't a file that needs backup; it must be personal to you. Make sure you use a simple password that is very strong. However, keep in mind that a strong password still doesn't make you completely safe.

GENERAL SAFETY TIPS

At this point, you should have an in-depth idea of what hacking is all about and some guidelines for ensuring the safety of your computer system or network. Following are general tips to follow to avoid becoming a victim of hackers.

· When you log into your email, you should avoid opening emails from unknown sources. Most importantly, do not download any attachments that come with such emails.

· Do not visit unsafe websites. Always visit websites that are secured, such as sites with "https". Try to only engage in safe browsing.

· Before you install a new program, make sure the program is scanned to ensure it is free of viruses. Then, you want to delete any old installation files because you now have the new installation files. This can save you if a hacker uses those old files as a backdoor.

· Scan your files from time to time. Also make sure that all of the applications on your system are updated frequently to the latest version.

· If you work at home, make sure you are in contact with security professionals or firms that can help you check network loopholes and rectify them as soon as possible.

· Always back up your files. You can use safe cloud drives such as Google Drive or Dropbox. You can also purchase an external drive to keep your important files safe and intact.

· Are you on a social network? Avoid clicking on links sent by people you don't know. Such tempting messages can be invitations to private chat rooms or promises of money if you click on the links. Avoid them and stay safe.

· As technology is improving, so are software developers. Always make sure you are surfing the internet with a good browser. For instance, some browsers have inbuilt virus or danger detection bots, which will alert you if you are trying to access a web page that is not safe. When you want to download a browser, go for one with better inbuilt security features. The following browsers are recommended:

a) Google Chrome

b) Mozilla Firefox

c) Safari

· Use the features that matter to you when you are connected to the internet with your browser. For instance, if you are not using Java or Active X while you are connected, deactivate them in your browser. Having them connected all the time is not safe.

· Research has shown that the most secure operating systems are Linux and Macintosh. If these two systems meet your needs, it is recommended that you switch to them. They are more secure, as they have had fewer incidences of hacking compared to the popular Windows systems.

· When you sleep, you can still be attacked if your computer system is on and idle or in sleep mode. To prevent this, make sure your computer is completely switched off when you are not using it.

Hacking with KAli Linux

Given all these features and modifications made to the Linux Debian system in order to make it useable for security testers and "white hats", the question now is, what makes Kali Linux the proper tool for a "white hat" hacker? One would think that due to its thorough security features and wide range of capabilities, that anyone would want to use Kali Linux. However, its specialized nature means exactly that; Kali Linux is designed specifically for professionals, for security specialists, penetration testers, and other types of "white hats". As such, Kali Linux offers little to no utility if the user wishes to have a Linux distribution that is for general – purpose use, or a specialized distribution for development, design, gaming, and Kali Linux is especially not recommended for beginner users of Linux.

Note as well that while Kali Linux is a type of open – source software, it's not entirely widely open – source, mainly for security reasons. Thus, the development team is kept small, with packages and repositories signed by each team member that uploaded it as well as the team as a whole for verification and security purposes, and the amount of upstream repositories used are kept to a minimum, with as few updates and packages drawn from them as possible, again all in the interest of security. This configuration means that adding new repositories or packages that have not been fully vetted by the Kali Linux team is wont to cause problems and may just break the installation of Kali Linux. Though as discussed earlier, Kali Linux was designed and intended to allow for a very high degree of user customization, the user still has to know what packages and repositories are compatible with Kali Linux, as adding unrelated or unvetted packages or software repositories will still most likely lead to bugs. For example, while Kali Linux has a lot of features, it does not support the apt – add – repository command, PPAs, or Launchpad, showing exactly the intent of the developers. Other unrelated programs such as Steam will also most likely not end well, and the Kali Linux distribution will most likely not work out well if that is the user's intent.

Even the insertion of some mainstream software packages such as NodeJS can take a bit of effort and know – how, but then, what Linux distribution doesn't? However, due to the advanced nature of Kali Linux, it would require more than just a basic level of sys – ad competence in order to make proper use of and unlock the full potential of the Kali Linux distribution. This is also another reason why Kali Linux is not recommended for beginners, as the specialized nature means that it is difficult to learn from scratch, and as it is highly specialized, the knowledge that one may pick up from learning Kali Linux may not be applicable to other Linux distributions as a whole.

Last but not least is that due to the fact that Kali Linux was developed as a "white hat" tool, and contains numerous security and penetration testing tools, it may be possible that these tools may be used improperly if the user is not quite familiar with what they are doing. Misuse of these tools, especially on a network where the user was not given express authorization, may result in damage, either to the system or the network, and may also result in numerous consequences, be it personal or legal. Take note that while this is the reason for network services being deactivated by default, if something happens, "not knowing what I did" is not a valid excuse, and an inexperienced user may just find themselves landing in hot water.

However, for professional penetration testers or "white hats", or even for those who are still studying or practicing with the aim of becoming a professional, Kali Linux has one of the best and most expansive toolkits available, especially at its price point – free.

Chapter 3) Text Manipulation

Phishing is a popular web attack used by both scammers and hackers. By pretending to be an authentic and trusted authority, it manipulates the victim into giving out personal information. The hacker can achieve this by pretending to be a representative of an IT company or bank, an employee of an online payment system or even a friend from a social media website. Phishing is a social engineering attack technique. It attempts to pull a user to a website that is often a clone of an original website with which the user is familiar or that the user visits frequently.

Phishing is usually achieved by cloning a legitimate website in the hopes of getting the user's login details. The website is cloned to look exactly like the original website; a piece of code is written that collects the username and password used on the website. That information is then saved in a remote location, usually in text format. Next, this cloned website uses the user's login credentials to create a login attempt on the original site so the user will be logged into the original website. This is a very important step in the phishing procedure, as it is essential that the victim does not suspect foul play during his or her attempt at logging into the website.

The user is also cajoled into visiting the cloned website through the use of a phishing email that prompts the user into clicking a link that redirects the user to the cloned website. The Social Engineering Toolkit in Kali Linux is an important tool in achieving this feat. The social engineering tool contains options for cloning a website exactly as it is on the original website. It also contains a tool for sending the mass email to several target email addresses or to a single target email address.

To execute a phishing attack effectively, you must log into your Kali Linux distro, click the application icon, go to BackTrack and choose the Exploitation Tools option on the right. This will display another set of options containing tools like Web Exploitation tools and Physical Exploitation tools. Our focus will be on clicking the Social Engineering tools. We choose the Social Engineering Toolkit. The Social Engineering Toolkit will open the terminal and show a menu containing different social engineering attack tools. We choose the Web Attack Vector option, then choose the credential harvester attack method on option 3. This option would allow us to clone a website.

The credential harvester option opens up a menu containing three options: (1) the web template option which allows the social engineering tool to import a set of pre-defined web applications we can use in the attack; (2) the site cloner, which helps us clone any site of our choosing; and (3) importing our own customized HTML template. Option two would make the Social Engineering Toolkit ask for the IP address on which to listen and for the website to be cloned. Once these two parameters are provided, the toolkit starts cloning the website. When an unsuspecting victim visits this website, the SET collects the username and password. The website clone is typically used with the spear-phishing option, in which the link to the cloned website is sent in a mass email attack to several targets or to just one target.

Keyloggers are scripts or devices that allow the hacker to track each keyboard or keypad stroke of the victim and save it in a text or readable format. It is a very useful tool for information gathering. Often, keyloggers are programs or scripts that run in the background on the computer on which they are installed, although physical keyloggers exist as USB multiports or as P2S ports to which the keyboard is connected before being connected to the CPU. This type of physical keylogger contains a memory chip that can be removed and checked for all the information and keyboard strokes it has stored. There are also wireless keyloggers that can sniff, intercept and hijack data sent from a keyboard to its receiver. In addition, there is keylogger software that is installed on the target computer. This type of keylogger software runs in the background without interfering with the victim's activity on his or her personal computer.

Software-based keyloggers must be installed on the victim's computer. This can be done in various ways, which we will discuss shortly. A hacker may be aware of a flaw present in an app the client uses and then exploit this vulnerability to trick the victim into visiting a website that downloads and executes the keylogger. The hacker may send the victim links to download an app or file containing the keylogger. When the victim installs this application, it runs the keylogger installation in the background and starts the keylogger program. A hacker may, on the other hand, place the keylogger in a USB drive with an autorun file. When an individual pick up this drive and inserts it into his/her computer, curious about what is on the drive, the keylogger is automatically executed in the background and starts tracking the user's keystrokes. Most of these types of keyloggers work remotely and need an internet connection to send the key logs to the hacker. Other types of keyloggers save the keystrokes locally on the victim's computer and require the hacker to have physical access to the computer to retrieve the log files. Keyloggers are also capable of doing more than tracking keystrokes. They can take screenshots and save information copied on the screen and copied to the clipboard.

Keyloggers are powerful programs. They are easy to build, and most are executed as part of a rootkit. Spyware like keyloggers are very powerful and require minimal coding and resources to run on the operating system. They can fly under the radar and be undetectable by the system's antivirus application. They typically consist of a dynamic link library and an installer which installs these files and enables them to run in the background. The keylogger can be created using the Metaspoilt option in Kali Linux with the meterpreter. The keyscan_start command is used to start up the keylogger, while the keyscan_dump command requests and receives the log files of the keyboard strokes.

Protection against keyloggers is recommended for any PC user. A good way to do this is by installing antispyware on the computer system. Keyloggers can be very sneaky and can avoid detection by the antivirus software on a PC. The spyware tool would search and pick out keyloggers running in the background. Some antispyware also encrypts the keystroke of the keyboard, causing the keylogger to send a jumbled-up logfile to the remote hacker. This encryption technique is also useful against hardware keyloggers. Although there is no one-size-fits-all approach to protection against keyloggers, it is advisable to regularly scan the system, check background processes for odd processes running in the background and avoid downloading and installing suspicious applications.

Chapter 4) Basic Kali Linux tools

In this section we will go through the various tools available in Kali Linux for security and penetration testing. There are a number of tools in Kali which are classified as per the task that they are used for. They are as follows.

    1. Exploitation Tools

2. Forensics Tools

3. Information Gathering Tools

4. Reverse Engineering tools

5. Wireless Attack Tools

6. Reporting Tools

7. Stress Testing Tools

8. Maintaining Access Tools

9. Sniffing and Spoofing Tools

10.   Password Attack Tools

We will go through tools available on Kali Linux for all the categories one by one and understand the purpose of each tool and how it will help us in the security domain.

Exploitation Tools

On a network of computers, usually over the Internet, there are several web applications, which leave a system vulnerable due to bad code or open ports on the server which are publicly accessible. Exploitation tools help you to target a system and exploit the vulnerabilities in that system, thus helping you to patch a vulnerability. Let's go through all the Exploitation Tools available in Kali Linux one at a time.

Armitage

Armitage was developed by Raphael Mudge to be used with the Metasploit framework as its GUI frontend. Armitage is a tool that recommends exploits and is fairly simple to use as cyber-attack management tool which is available in the graphical form. It is open source and available for free security tool and is mostly known for the data it provides on shared sessions and the communication it provides through a single instance of Metasploit. Armitage helps a user to launch exploits and scans, get recommendations of exploits and explore the advanced features that are available in the Metasploit framework.

The Backdoor Factory (BDF)

The Backdoor Factory is a tool commonly used by researchers and security professionals. This tool allows a user to include his desirable code in executable binaries of a system or an application and continue execution of the binaries in normal state as if there was no additional code added to it.

You can install this tool on your Kali Linux system using the following commands on the terminal.

apt-getupdate

apt-getinstallbackdoor-factory

The Browser Exploitation Framework (BeEF)

The Browser Exploitation Framework is penetration testing tool built for testing exploits on the web browser. There has been an observation wherein web browsers have been targeted using vulnerabilities on the client-side. BeEF helps the user analyse these attack vectors on the client side. Unlike other tools, BeEF focuses on assessing the Web Browser which serves as an open door and it looks past the network layer and client's system.

Commix

Providing use cases for penetration tester, web developers, and researchers, Commix (short for COMMand Injection eXploiter) works in a simple environment to test web applications. It basically allows a user to find the errors, bugs or vulnerabilities with respect to command injections in web applications. This tool easily allows you to identify and exploit a vulnerability of command injection. The Commix tool has been developed using the Python language.

Crackle

The Crackle tool in Kali Linux is a brute force utility used for cracking and intercepting traffic between bluetooth devices. Most bluetooth devices have a 4-6 digit pairing code, which is in an encrypted format. Using Crackle, these codes can be decrypted if the pairing process between 2 devices is intercepted and thus allowing you to listen to all communication happening between the 2 devices.

jboss-autopwn

JBoss Autopwn is a penetration testing tool used in JBoss applications. The Github version of JBoss Autopwn is outdated and the last update is from 2011. It is a historical tool and not used much now.

Linux Exploit Suggester

The Linux Exploit Suggester tool provides a script that keeps track of vulnerabilities and shows all possible exploits that help a user get root access during a penetration test.

The script uses the uname -r command to find the kernel version of the Linux operating system. Additionally, it will also provide the -k parameter through which user can manually enter the version for the kernel of the Linux operating system.

Maltego Teeth

Maltego is a tool that is used for data mining and is interactive. It provides an interactive interface that outputs graphs which help in link analysis. Since it allows link analysis, Maltego is used for investigations on the Internet to find the relationship between information that is scattered over various web pages on the Internet. Maltego Teeth was developed later with an added functionality that gives penetration testers the ability to do password breaking, SQL injections and vulnerability detection, all using a graphical interface.

sqlmap

sqlmap is a Kali tool that is open source and is used for penetration testing. It allows automating the detection of SQL injection vulnerabilities and exploiting it to take over database servers. It comes equipped with a very powerful detection engine, a range of tools which will help an extreme penetration tester and switches that help fetch information like database fingerprinting, retrieving data from databases, access to the file system of the operating system and execute commands on the operating system.

Yersinia

Yersinia is a tool that detects exploits weaknesses in network protocols and takes advantage of it. It is a tool which is a solid framework for testing and analyzing deployment of networks and systems. It comprises of layer-2 attacks which exploit the weaknesses in various layer-2 protocols in a given network thus allowing a penetration tester to detect flaws in a layer-2 network. Yersinia is used during penetration tests to start attacks on network devices such as DHCP servers,switches, etc which use the spanning tree protocol.

Cisco-global-exploiter

The Cisco Global Exploiter (CGE) tool is a security testing exploit engine/tool, which is simple yet fast and advanced. Cisco switches and routers have 14 vulnerabilities which can be exploited using the Cisco Global Exploiter tool. The Cisco Global Exploiter is basically a perl script, which is driven using the command line and has a front-end that is simple and easy to use.

Cisco-torch

The Cisco Torch is an exploitation tool which varies from the regular scanners in the sense that it can be used to launch multiple and simultaneous scans at a given point in time which results in tasks getting done faster and more efficiently. In addition to the network layer, it also helps in fingerprinting systems in the application layer of the OSI model. This is something that even a tool like NMAP doesn't provide.

Forensics Tools

We will now list down and learn tools available in Kali Linux which are used in the Forensics domain.

Binwalk

The Binwalk tool is useful while working on binary image file. It lets you scan through the image file for executable code that may be embedded in the image file. It is a very powerful and useful tool for users who know what they are doing as it can be used to detect coveted information that is hidden in images of firmware. This can help in uncovering a loophole or a hack that is hidden in the image file, which is used with the intention to exploit the system.

The Binwalk tool is developed in python and makes use of the libmagic library from python, therefore making it an apt tool for magic signatures that are created for the Unix file system. To make it even more comfortable for testers in the investigation domain, it contains a database of signatures that are commonly found in firmware around the world. This makes it a convenient tool to detect anomalies.

Bulk-extractor

The bulk-extractor tool is an interesting tool used by investigators who want to fetch specific data from a digital file. The tools helps retrieve URLs, email addresses, credit/debit card numbers, etc. The tools can be used to scan through files, directories and even images of disks. The best part is that even if the data is corrupted partially or in a compressed format, the tool will still reach its depth to find the data.

Another interesting feature of this tool is that if there is data that you keep finding repeatedly, such as email addresses, URLs, you can create a search pattern for them, which can be displayed in the form of a histogram. It also ends up creating a list of words that are found in a given set of data that may be used to crack a password for files that have been encrypted.

Chkrootkit

The chkrootkit tool is usually used in a live boot scenario. It is used locally to check the host machine for any rootkits that may be installed on the host. It therefore helps in the hardening of a system, thus ensuring that the system is not compromised and vulnerable to a hacker.

The chkrootkit tool also has the ability to scan through system binaries for any modifications made to the rootkit, temporary deletion, string replacements, and latest log deletions made. These are just a few of the things that this little tool can do. It looks like a fairly simple tool but the power it possesses can be invaluable to a forensic investigator.

pOf

The pOf tool can help the user know the operating system of a host that is being targeted just by intercepting the transmitted packages and examining them and it does this irrespective of whether the targeted host is behind a firewall or not. The use of pOf does not lead to any increase in network traffic, no lookup of names, and no probes that may be found to be mysterious. Given all these features, pOf in the hands of an advanced user, can help detect presence of firewalls, use of NAT devices, and presence of load balancers as well.

pdf-parser

The pdf-parser tool is used in parsing PDF files to classify elements that are used in the file. The output of the tool on a PDF file will not be a PDF file. One may not recommend it for textbook cases of PDF parsers but it does help to get the job done. Mostly, its use case is PDF files, which you may suspect of being embedded with scripts in them.

Dumpzilla

The Dumpzilla tool is a tool that is developed in python. The purpose of this tool is to extract all information that may be of interest to forensics from web browsers like Seamonkey, Mozilla Firefox and Iceweasel.

ddrescue

The ddrescue tool is a savior of a tool. It helps in copying data from one block device such as a hard disc or a CD ROM to another block device. But the reason it is a savior is because it copies the good parts first to avoid any read errors on the source.

The ddrescue tool's basic operation is completely automatic which means that once you have started it, you do not need to wait for any prompts like an error, wherein you will need to stop the program or restart it.

By using the mapfule feature of the tool, data will be recovered in an efficient fashion as it will only read the blocks that are required. You also get the option to stop the ddrescue process at any time and resume it again later from the same point.

Foremost

Have you ever deleted files on purpose or by mistake and realized that you needed them later? The Foremost tool is there to your rescue. This tool is an open source package which is easy to use and helps you retrieve data off of disks that may have been formatted. It may not help recover the filename but the will recover the data it held. A magical feature is that even of the directory information is lost, it can help retrieve data by referencing to the header or footer of the file, making it a fast and reliable tool for data recovery.

An interesting piece of fact is that Foremost was developed by special agents of the US Air Force.

Galleta

The Galleta tool helps you parse a cookie trail that you have been following and convert it into a spreadsheet format, which can be exported for future reference.

Cookies can be evidence in a case of cyber-crime and it can be a challenging task to understand them in their original format. The Galleta tool comes handy here as it helps in structuring data that is retrieved from cookie trails, which then can be run through other software for deeper analysis. The inputs for this analysis software need the date to be in a spreadsheet format, which is where the Galleta tool proves to be very useful.

Volatility

When it comes to memory forensics, Volatility is a very popular tool. Developed in the python language, this tool facilitates the extraction of data from volatile memory such as RAM. It is compatible with 32 bit and 64 bit architectures of almost all Windows variants and limited flavors of Linux and Android. The tool accepts memory dumps in various formats such as crash dumps, raw memory dumps, hibernation files, virtual snapshots, etc. The tool allows you to get an idea of the run-time state of the host machine and is independent of the investigation of the host.

Password that are decrypted during run-time are stored in the RAM. Thus by retrieving the details of a password, Volatility comes as a savior for investigation of files that lie on the hard disk and may be encrypted with a password. This helps in decreasing the overall time that may be required for a particular case to be investigated.

Autopsy

Sleuth Kit is a digital forensics toolkit which is open source and can be used with a wide range of file systems such as FAT, NTFS, EXT2, EXT3(and raw images) to perform analysis that can be in depth. The graphical interface developed for Sleuth Kit (which is a command line tool) is called Autopsy. Autopsy brags of features such as Hash Filtering, Timeline analysis, File System analysis and searching for keywords. It is also very versatile as it lets you add other modules to the existing set for extended functionality.

You get the option to launch a fresh new case or use one which already exists when you launch the Autopsy tool.

Xplico

Xplico is a forensic tool, which is open source and is used for network forensics. If you wish to extract data from applications that use the network protocols or Internet, Xplico is the tool for you. All popular network protocols such as HTTPS, POP, SMTP, IMAP, SIP, UDP, TCP and others are supported by Xplico. It supports both IPv4 and IPv6. An SQLite database is used to store the output data from the tool.

Information Gathering Tools

The beginning of any attacks initiates from the stage of information gathering. When you gather as much information about the target, the attack becomes an easy process. Having information about the target also results in a higher success rate of the attack. A hacker finds all kinds of information to be helpful.

The process of information gathering includes:

Gathering information that will help in social engineering and ultimately in the attack

Understanding the range of the network and computers that will be the targets of the attack

Identifying and understanding all the complete surface of the attack i.e. processes and systems that are exposed

Identifying the services of a system that are exposed, and collecting as much information about them as possible

Querying specific service that will help fetch useful data such as usernames

We will now go through Information Gathering tools available in Kali Linux one by one.

Nmap and Zenman

Ethical hacking is a phase in Kali Linux for which the tools NMap and ZenMap are used. NMap and ZenMap are basically the same tool. ZenMap is a Graphical Interface for the NMap tool which works on the command line.

The NMap tool which is for security auditing and discovery of network is a free tool. Apart from penetration testers, it is also used by system administrators and network administrators for daily tasks such as monitoring the uptime of the server or a service and managing schedules for service upgrades.

NMap identifies available hosts on a network by using IP packets which are raw. This also helps NMap identify the service being hosted on the host which includes the name of the application and the version. Basically, the most important application it helps identify on a network is the filter or the firewall set up on a host.

Stealth Scan

The Stealth scan is also popularly known as the hal open scan or SYN. It is called the half open scan because it refrains from completing the usual three-way handshake of TCP. So how it works is a SYN packet is sent by an attacker to the target host. The target host will acknowledge the SYN and sent a SYN/ACK in return. If a SYN/ACK is received, it can be safely assumed that the connection to the target host will complete and the port is open and listening on the target host. If the response received is RST instead, it is safe to assume that the port is close or not active on the target host.

acccheck

The acccheck tool was developed has an attack tool consisting of a password dictionary to target Windows Authentication processes which use the SMB protocol. The accccheck is basically a wrapper script which is injected in the binary of 'smbclient' and therefore depends on the smbclient binary for execution.

Server Message Block (SMB) protocol is an implementation of Microsoft for file sharing over a network and is popularly known as the Microsoft SMB Protocol.

Amap

Amap is a scanning too of the next generation that allows a good number of options and flags in its command line syntax making it possible to identify applications and processes even if the ports that they are running on are different.

For example, a web server by default accepts connections on port 80. But most companies may change this port to something else such as 1253 to make the server secure. This change would be easily discovered by Amap.

Furthermore, if the services or applications are not based on ASCII, Amap is still able to discover them. Amap also has a set of interesting tools, which have the ability to send customized packets which will generate specific responses from the target host.

Amap, unlike other network tools is not just a simple scanner, which was developed with the intention of just pinging a network to detect active hosts on the network. Amap is equipped with amapcrap, which is a module that sends bogus and completely random data to a port. The target port can be UDP, TCP, SSL, etc. The motive is to force the target port to generate a response.

CaseFile

CaseFile is known as the younger sibling of Maltego. Casefile has the same ability as Maltego to create graphs but it cannot run transforms on it. Although, you can quickly add data and then link and analyze it using CaseFile. The CaseFile tool is for investigators who work on data that is fetched from offline sources since the data they require can be queried by automation or programming. These are investigators who are getting their data from other team members and are using that data to build an information map based on their investigation.

A huge number of Maltegousers were using Maltego to try and build graphical data from offline investigations and that is how CaseFile was born. Since there was no need of the transform provided by Maltego and the real need was just the graphing capability of Maltego in and more flexible way, CaseFile was developed.

CaseFile, being an application of visual intelligence, helps to determine the relationships, connections and links in the real world between information of different types. CaseFile lets you understand the connections between data that may apart from each other by multiple degrees of separation by plotting the relationships between them graphically. Additionally, CaseFile comes bundled with many more entities that are useful in investigations making it a tool that is efficient. You can also add your custom entities to CaseFile, which allows you to extend this tool to your own custom data sets.

braa

Braa is a tool that is used for scanning mass Simple Network Management Protocol (SNMP). The tool lets you make SNMP queries, but unlike other tools which make single queries at a time to the SNMP service, braa has the capability to make queries to multiple hosts simultaneously, using one single process. The advantage of braa is that it scans multiple hosts very fast and that too by using very limited system resources.

Unlike other SNMP tools, which require libraries from SNMP to function, braa implements and maintains its own stack of SNMP. The implementation is very complex and dirty. Supports limited data types and cannot be called up to standard in any case. However, braa was developed to be a fast tool and it is fast indeed.

dnsmap

dnsmap is a tool that came into existence originally in 2006 after being inspired from the fictional story "The Thief No One Saw" by Paul Craig.

A tool used by penetration testers in the information gathering stage, dnsmap helps discover the IP of the target company, domain names, netblocks, phone numbers, etc.

Dnsmap also helps on subdomain brute forcing which helps in cases where zone transfers of DNS do not work. Zone transfers are not allowed publicly anymore nowadays which makes dnsmap the need of the hour.

DotDotPwn

The dotdotpwn tool can be defined simply to call it a fuzzer. What is a fuzzer? A fuzzer is a testing tool that targets software for vulnerabilities by debugging and penetrating through it. It scans the code and looks for flaws and loopholes, bad data, validation errors, parameters that may be incorrect and other anomalies of programming.

Whenever an anomaly is encountered by the software, the software may become unresponsive, making way for the flaws to give an open door to an attack. For example, if you are an attacker whose target is a company's web server, with the help of dotdotpwn, you will be able to find a loophole in the code of the web server. Perhaps there has been a latest HTTP update on the server overnight. Using a fuzzer on the web server shows you there is an exploit with respect to data validation which leaves an open door for a DoS attack. You can now exploit this vulnerability, which will make the server crash and server access will be denied to genuine employees of the company. There are many such errors that can be discovered using a fuzzer and it is very common for technology to have error when it releases something new in the market and it takes time to identify the error and fix it.

Another example would be an attack with respect to SQL called SQLi where 'i' stands for injection. SQL injection attacks are achieved by injecting SQL database queries through web forms that are available on a website. The conclusion is that software will always be vulnerable allowing attackers to find a way to break their way into the system.

Fierce

Fierce is a Kali tool which is used to scan ports and map networks. Discovery of hostnames across multiple networks and scanning of IP spaces that are non-contiguous can be achieved by using Fierce. It is a tool much like Nmap but in case of Fierce, it is used specifically for networks within a corporate.

Once the target network has been defined by a penetration tester, Fierce runs a whole lot of tests on the domains in the target network and retrieves information that is valuable and which can be analyzed and exploited by the attacker.

Fierce has the following features.

- Capabilities for a brute-force attack through custom and built-in test list

- Discovery of nameservers

- Zone transfer attacks

- Scan through IP ranges both internal and external

- Ability to modify the DNS server for reverse host lookups

Wireshark

Wireshark is a kali too that is an open source analyzer for network and works on multiple platforms such as Linux, BSD, OS X and Windows.

It helps one understand about the functioning of a network thus making it of use in government infrastructure, education industries and other corporates.

It is similar to the tcpdump tool, but WIreshark is a notch above as it has a graphical interface through which you can filter and organize the data that has been captured, which means that it takes less time to analyze the data further. There is also an only text based version known as tshark, which has almost the same amount of features.

Wireshark has the following features.

- The interface has a user-friendly GUI
- Live capture of packets and offline analysis
- Support for Gzip compression and extraction
- Inspection of full protocol
- Complete VOiP analysis
- Supports decryption for IPsec, Kerberos, SSL/TLS, WPA/WPA2

URLCrazy

URLCrazy is a Kali tool that can that tests and generates typos and variations in domains to target and perform URL hijacking, typo squatting and corporate espionage. It has a database that can generate variants of up to 15 types for domains, and misspellings of up to 8000 common spellings. URLCrazy supports a variety of keyboard layouts, checks if a particular domain is in use and figures how popular a typo is.

The Harvester

The Harvester is a Kali tool that is not your regular hacking tool. Whenever there is a mention of hacking tools that are implemented using the command line, one usually thinks of tools like Nmap, Reaver, Metasploit and other utilities for wireless password cracking. However, the harvester refrains from using algorithms that are advanced to break into firewalls, or crack passwords, or capture the data of the local network.

Instead, the Harvester simply gathers publicly available information such as employee names, email addresses, banners, subdomains and other information in the same range. You may wonder as to why it collects this data. Because this data is very useful in the primary stage of information gathering. All this data helps study and understand the target system which makes attacking easier for the hacker or the penetration tester.

Furthermore, it helps the attacker understand as to how big and Internet footprint the target has. It also helps organizations to know how much publicly available information their employees have across the Internet. The latest version of the Harvester has updates which lets it keep intervals between the requests it makes to pages on the Internet, improves search sources, plotting of graphs and statistics, etc.

The Harvester crawls through the Internet as your surrogate, looking for information on your behalf as long as the criteria provided by you matches the information on the Internet. Given that you can also gather email addresses using the Harvester, this tool can be very useful to a hacker who is trying to penetrate an online login by gaining access to the email account of an individual.

Metagoofil

Metagoofil is a kali tool that is aimed at fetching publicly available such as pdf, xls, doc, ppt, etc. documents of a company on the Internet.

The tool makes a Google search to scan through documents and download them to the local machine. It then extracts the metadata of the documents using libraries such as pdfminer, hachoir, etc. It then feeds the information gathering process with the results of its report which contains usernames, server or machine names and software version which helps penetration testers with their investigation.

Miranda

Miranda is a Kali tool that is actively or passively used to detect UPnP hosts, its services, its devices and actions, all through on single command. The Service state parameters and their associated actions are correlated automatically and are then processed as input/output variables for every action. Miranda uses a single data structure to store information of all the hosts and allows you access to that data structure and all its contents.

Let's discuss what exactly ÚPnP is. Universal Plug and Play or UPnP is a protocol for networking that allows devices on the network such as computers, printers, routers mobile devices, etc. to discover each other seamlessly over a network and established services between them for sharing of data, entertainment and other communication. It is ideally for networks inside a private residence as opposed to corporate infrastructure.

Ghost Phisher

Ghost Phisher is a Kali tool, which is used as an attack software program and also for security auditing of wired and wireless networks. It is developed using the Python programming language and the Python GUI library. The program basically emulates access points of a network therefore, deploying its own internal server into a network.

Fragroute

Fragroute is a Kali tool that is used for intercepting, modifying and rewriting traffic that is moving toward a specific host. Simply put, the packets from attacking system known as frag route packets are routed to the destination system. It is used for bypassing firewalls mostly by attackers and security personnel. Information gathering is a well-known use case for fragroute as well which used by penetration testers who use a remote host, which is highly secured.

Masscan

Masscan is a Kali tool, which is used by penetration testers all around the world and has been in the industry for a long time. It is a tool of reconnaissance which has the capability to transmit up to 10 million packets every second. The transmission used by masscan is asynchronous and it has custom stack of TCP/IP. Therefore, the threads used for sending and receiving packets are unique.

Masscan is used to simultaneously attack a large number of hosts and that too quickly. The tool developer claims that masscan can scan the entire Internet in 6 minutes. Given its super high transmission rate, it has a use case in the domain of stress testing as well.

However, to achieve those high transmission rates, special drives and NICs are required. The communication of the tool with the users is very similar to that between the user and the Nmap tool. Feature of masscan are as follows.

- It can be used to enumerate the whole Internet
- It can be used to enumerate a huge number of hosts
- Various subnets within an organization can be enumerated
- It can be used for random scanning and fun on the Internet

Reverse Engineering tools

We can learn how to make and break things from something as simple as a Lego toy to a car engine simply by dismantling the parts one by one and then putting them back together. This process wherein we break things down to study it deeply and further improves it is called Reverse Engineering.

The technique of Reverse Engineering in its initial days would only be used with hardware. As the process evolved over the years, engineers started applying it to software, and now to human DNA as well. Reverse engineering, in the domain of cyber security helps understand that if a system was breached, how the attacker entered the system and the steps that he took to break and enter into the system.

While getting into the network of a corporate infrastructure, attackers endure that they are utilizing all the tools available to them in the domain of computer intrusion tools. Most of the attackers are funded and skilled and have a specific objective for an attack towards which they are highly motivated. Reverse Engineering empowers us to put up a fight against such attackers in the future. Kali Linux comes equipped with a lot of tools that are useful in the process of reverse engineering in the digital world. We will list down some of these tools and learn their use.

Apktool

Apktool is a Kali Linux tool that is used in the process of reverse engineering. This tool has the ability to break down resources to a form that is almost the original form and then recreate the resource by making adjustments. It can also debug code that is small in size,step by step. It has a file structure, which is project-like, thus making it easy to work with an app. Using apktool you can also automate tasks that are repetitive in nature like the building of an apk.

Dex2jar

Dex2jar is a Kali tool which is a lightweight API and was developed to work with the Dalvik Executable that is the .dex/.odex file formats. The tool basically helps to work with the .class files of Java and Android.

It has the following components.

-        Dex2jar has an API, which is lightweight similar to that of ASM.

-        dex-translator component does the action of converting a job. It reads instructions from dex to the dex-ir format and converts it to ASM format after optimizing it.

-        Dex-ir component, which is used by the dex-translator component basically represents the dex instructions.

- dex-tools component works with the .class files. It is used for tasks such as modifying an apk, etc.

diStorm3

diStorm is a Kali tool which is an easy to use decomposer library and is lightweight at the same time. Instructions can be disassembled in 16 bit, 32 bit and 64 bit modes using diStorm. It is also popular amongst penetration testers as it is the fast disassembler library. The source code, which depends on the C library is very clean, portable, readable and independent of a particular platform which allows it to be used in embedded modules and kernel modules.

diStorm3 is the latest version which is backward compatible with diStorm64's old interface. However, using the new header files is essential.

edb-debugger

edb debugger is a Kali tool which is the Linux equivalent for the popular Windows tool called "Olly debugger." It is a debugging tool with modularity as one of its main goals. Some of its features are as follows.

- An intuitive Graphical User InterfaceI
- All the regular debugging operations such as step-into, step-over, run and break
- Breakpoints for conditions

- Basic analysis for instructions
- View or Dump memory regions
- Address inspection which is effective
- Generation and import of symbol maps
- Various available plugins
- The core that is used for debugging is integrated as a plugin so that it can be replaced when needed as per requirement.
- The view of the data dump is in tabbed format. This feature allows the user to open several views of the memory at a given time while allowing you to switch between them

Jad Debugger

Jad is a Kali Linux tool that is a Java decompiler and the most popular one in the world. It is a tool, which runs on the command line and is written in the C++ language. Over the years, there have been many graphical interfaces which have been developed which run Jad in the background and provide a comfortable front end to the users to perform tasks such as project management, source browsing, etc. Kali Linux powers Jad in its releases to be used for Java application debugging and other processes of reverse engineering.

Javasnoop

JavaSnoop is a tool developed by Aspect Security tool for Kali Linux that allows testing of Java application security. By developing JavaSnoop, Aspect has proved how it is a leader in the security industry in providing verification services for all applications and not just web based applications.

JavaSnoop allows you to begin tampering with method calls, run customized code or sit back and see what's going on the system by just attaching an existing process such as a debugger.

OllyDbg

OllyDbg is a Kali Linux tool, which is a debugger at a level of a 32 bit Assembler developed for Microsoft Windows. What makes it particularly useful is its emphasis on code that is in binary in times when the source is not available.

OllyDbg brags of the following features.

- Has an interactive user interface and no command line hassle

- Loads and debugs DLLs directly

- Allows function descriptions, comments and labels to be defined by the user

- No trash files in the registry or system directories post installation

- Can be used to debug multi threaded applications
- Many third party applications can be integrated as it has an open architecture
- Attaches itself to running programs

Valgrind

Valgrind is a tool in Kali Linux tool, which is used for profiling and debugging Linux based systems. The tool allows you to manage threading bugs and memory management bugs automatically. It helps eliminate hours that one would waste on hunting down bugs and therefore, stabilizes the program to a very great extent. A program's processing speed can be increased by doing a detailed profiling on the program by using Valgrind too.suite for debugging and profiling Linux programs. The Valgrind distribution has the following production quality tools currently.

- Memcheck which detects errors in memory
- DRD and Helgrind which are two other thread error detectors
- Cachegrind which is a branch prediction and cache profiling tool
- Callgrind which branch detection profile and a call graph generating cache profiler
- Massif which profiles heaps

Three experimental tools are also included in the Valgrind distribution

-      SGCheck which detector for stack or global array overrun

-      DHAT which is a second profiler for heap and helps understand how heap blocks are being used

-      BBV which basic block vector generator

Reverse Engineering plays an important role where manufacturers are using it to sustain competition from rivals. Other times reverse engineering is used to basically figure out flaws in software and re-build a better version of the software. Kali Linux provides tools, which are known in the reverse engineering domain. In addition tools that we have discussed, there are many 3rd party reverse engineering tools as well but the ones we have discussed come installed in the Kali Linux image.

Wireless Attack Tools

In this chapter, we will look at various tools that are available in Kali Linux, which can be used for penetrating wireless devices and other devices which are accessible through wireless networks.

Aircrack

Aircrack is a Kali Linux tool, which is used for cracking passwords wirelessly and is the most popular tool in the world for what it does. It is used for cracking keys of 802.11 WEP and WPA-PSK around the world. It tries to figure out the password from the packets that are being transmitted by analyzing the packets that were caught by it initially. It can also recover the password or crack the password of a network by implementing FMS attacks that are standard in nature by optimizing the attack to some extent. PTW attacks and KoreK attacks are some of the optimizations used as make the attack work faster than other tools, which are used for cracking WEP passwords. Aircrack is a very powerful tool and is used the most all over the world.

The interface it offers is in console format. The company that has manufactured Aircrack offers online tutorials to get hands on experience.

AirSnort

AirSnort is another Kali Linux tool which is used for cracking passwords of wireless LANS and is very popular. Wi-Fi802.11b network's WEP keys can be cracked by using AirSnort. This tool basically monitors the packets that are being transmitted on the network passively. When it has sufficient packets, it computes the encryption key from the packets it has gathered. AirSnort is available for free on both Linux and Windows platforms and is fairly simple to use as well. The tool has not seen any development or updates in 3 years but the company, which created the tool is now looking to develop and maintain it further. The tool due to its direct involvement in cracking WEP is popular around the globe. ***Kismet***

Kismet is another Kali Linux tool, which is basically used in troubleshooting issues on wireless networks. It can be used with any wi-fi device, which supports rfmon, which is a monitoring mode. It is available on most of the platforms, which include Linux, Windows, OS X and other BSD platforms. Kismet again collects packets passively to understand the network standard and can also detect networks that are hidden in nature. It is built on the client-server architecture and it can sniff traffic from802.11b, 802.11a, 802.11g, and 802.11n. It supports the recent wireless standards, which are faster as well.

Cain & Able

Cain & Able is Kali Linux tool that is popular amongst penetration testers for its ability to crack wireless networks. The tool was originally developed to intercept traffic on a network. Later developments turned it into a tool, which could brute force its way into cracking passwords of wireless networks. The tool analyzes routing protocols of a network and helps in finding the passwords of the network. This is another popular tool used for cracking wireless network passwords. This tool was developed to intercept the network traffic and then use the brute forcing to discover the passwords.

Fern WiFi Wireless Cracker

Fern Wi-Fi Wireless Cracker is another Kali Linux tool that is very helpful with respect to network security. The tool helps you identify hosts by monitoring all network traffic in real time. The tool was initially developed to detect flaws on networks and fix the flaws that were detected. The tool is available on Linux, Windows and Apple platforms.

CoWPAtty

CoWPAtty is another Kali Linux too that is used for cracking passwords of wireless networks. It cracks passwords of the WPA-PSK networks using an automated dictionary attack. It maintains a database, which contains thousands of passwords which it uses during the attack. The chances of the tool cracking the password are very high if the password is there in its database. The drawback is that the speed of the tool can be slow and it depends on the password strength and the number of words in its database. The fact that the tool uses SHA1 algorithm with a seed of SSID is another reason for its slow speed. What this means is that thee SSIM of the password will be different. Thus the rainbow table of the tool may be ineffective while being used for the access points. Therefore, for each word that is being used for the SSID, the password dictionary of the tool generates a hash for each word. The tool is fairly simple to use with a list of commands that are to be used.

The newer versions of CoWPAtty use hash files which are pre computed and therefore the time used for computation during the process of cracking is brought down significantly, resulting in increasing the speed of the process. The hash file which is pre computed already contains 172000 dictionary files which contain at least 1000 of the most popular SSIDs. It is important for your SSID to be in that list for the attack to be successful. If the SSID is not in that list, you are just plain unlucky.

Airjack

Airjack is a Kali Linux too which is used for packet injection in Wi-Fi 802.11. DOS and MIM attacks are a specialty of this tool. This tool forces the network to give a denial of service by injecting bogus packets into the network. The tool can also help create a man in the middle attack in a given network. The tool is both powerful and popular among users.

WepAttack

WepAttack is another Kali Linux tool built on open source platform for breaking keys of 802.11 WEP. It maintains a dictionary of millions of words, which it uses to crack the password of a network. The only requirement to perform an attack using WepAttack is a WLAN card that is in a working condition. The usability of WepAttack is very limited but it works amazingly well on WLAN cards that are supported.

Wifiphisher

Wifiphisher is a Kali Linux tool, which is again used to crack the password of a wireless network. The tool steals passwords of a wireless network by executing fast paced phishing attacks. Kali Linux has Wifiphisher pre-installed on it. It is a tool that is available on Linux, Windows and MAC and completely free to use.

Reaver

Reaver is an open-source Kali Linux tool, which is used for creating attacks which are brute force in nature against WPS. The tool is used to crack the passwords WPA/WPA2 encryptions. The tool is hosted on code developed by Google and there are high chances that the tool will be taken down if there is no local backup made for it. The last time Reaver was updated was about 4 years ago. It is a good to have tool, in addition to all the other password cracking tools that a penetration tester may want to have as it uses the same attack method.

Wifite

Wifite is also a Kali Linux tool which helps crack networks that are encrypted with WPS via reaver. It works on all Linux based operating systems. Many features related to cracking passwords are offered by Wifite.

WepDecrypt

WepDecrypt is Kali Linux tool written in C language to target wireless networks. It performs a dictionary attack and tries to guess WEP keys. Additionally it also uses key generators and performs distributed network attacks and other methods to figure out the key of a wireless network. It depends on a few libraries to function. It i snot a very popular tool among users but advisable for beginners to understand the functions of dictionary attacks.

CommonView for Wi-Fi

CommonView for Wi-Fi is Kali Linux tool, which is a network monitor for wireless networks and also used for analyzing packets. It is a simple tool, which comes with a graphical user interface that is easy to understand. The tool was developed for wireless network admins and security professionals who are interested in monitoring and troubleshooting problems related to wireless networks. The tool works with Wi-Fi 802.11 a/b/g/n/ac networks. The tool comfortably captures every packet and lets you view the network information. It also gives you other information like access points, protocol distribution, signal strength etc. The tools provides valuable information about a wireless network and comes across as a handy tool for network administrators.

Pyrit

Pyrit is also a very good Kali Linux tool which allows you to attack lets you perform attack IEEE 802.11 WPA/WPA2-PSK encrypted wireless networks. This is a freely available tool, which is hosted on Google Code. Again since it is hosted by Google, it may be taken off in the coming months and therefore, it is good to have a local copy of it. It supports a wide range of operating systems such as Linux, OS X, FreeBSD, etc. It cracks WPS/WPA-2 passwords using the brute force attack method. Being very effective, it is suggested that everyone tries this tool out at least once.

Reporting Tools

The report you get as a result of the penetration test that you have conducted is a key deliverable in an activity carried out for security assessment. The final deliverable of penetration testing is the report, which gives a record of the service that was provided, the methods that were used, the findings or results of the tests and the recommendations that come as an output to better the security. Report making is most of the times ignored as it is found to be boring by many penetration testers. In this part, we will talk about the Kali Linux tools that are available to make the process of making reports simple. The tools help you store your penetration test results, which can be referred to when you are working on making the report. The tools will also help you communicate and share data with your team.

We are covering the 2 main tools, which are Dradis and Magic Tree.

Dradis

The Dradis framework is an open source Kali tool which functions as a platform to collaborate and report for security exports in the network security domain. The tool is developed in Ruby language and is independent of platform. Dradis provides the option to export reports and all the activities can be recorded in one single report. Exporting the report in file formats that are PDF or DOC is currently only supported in the pro version and is missing from the community version.

Magic Tree

Magic Tree is a Kali Linux tool, which is used for reporting and data management and it is much like Dradis. It is designed in a way such that data consolidation, execution of external commands, querying and generation of reports becomes an easy and straightforward process. Kali Linux has this tool pre-installed and it is located at "Reporting Tools" category. It manages the host and its associated data using the tree node structure.

Magic Tree vs. Dradis

Both Magic Tree and Dradis have been designed to solve the same set of problems i.e. data consolidation and report generation. Both Magic Tree and Dradis allow data to be imported from that which is produced by various tools used for penetration testing. It also allows data to be added manually and report generation of that data. The tree structure is followed by both the tools to store data.

Stress Testing Tools

Stress testing can be defined as a software testing methodology, which is carried out to find out the reliability and stability of a system. The test makes a system go through extreme conditions to find out how robust it can be how efficiently is can handle the errors under such circumstances.

Stress tests are designed to test systems even beyond the regular points of operation to understand how well it can handle pressure. Stress testing was introduced to ensure that a system, which is in production would not crash under extreme situations.

Let us see the various stress testing tools that are available in Kali Linux.

DHCPig

DHCPig is a Kali Linux tool that exhausts the DHCP server system by initiating an exhaustion attack on it. This tool will use up all the IPs available on the network and stop new users from being assigned any IPs, release IPs that have been already assigned to genuine devices, and then for a good amount of time, it will send out gratuitous ARP and kick all the Windows hosts from the network. The tool requires admin privileges and scapy >=2.1 library to execute. The tool does not need any configuration as such, and you just have to pass the environment as a parameter on which you plan to release the test. It has been successfully tested on multiple DHCP server in Windows and on several Linux distributions.

inviteflood

Inviteflood is a Kali Linux tool, which is used to send SIP/SDP INVITE message to cause a flooding over UDP/IP.

It has been tested over several Linux platforms and it performs well on all distributions.

mdk3

MSK is a Kali Linux too which is proof-of-concept tool used to exploit the protocol weaknesses of IEEE 802.11

Note: Ensure that the network owner has permitted you to run MDK on it before you run it on the network.

FunkLoad

FunkLoad is a Kali Linux too that web tester for functions and load on a system. It is developed in Python and has the following use cases.

Testing web projects for their functionality and regression testing as well.

Test the performance of the web application by applying load on it. This helps to understand bottlenecks and helps you to get a detailed report of the test.

Primary testing like volume testing or longevity testing would not result in showing bugs that would show up on load testing. This is achieved through FunkLoad.

It is a stress testing tool which will end up overwhelming a web application and its resources. This also helps in understanding the recoverability of the application.

You can also write scripts to automate repetitive tasks.

ipv6-toolkit

The IPV6 toolkit by SI6 Network is a set of tools to test the security of IPv6 networks and troubleshoot any problems that arise on it. You can perform real-time attacks on an IPv6 network which will help you assess the security, resiliency, and will help you troubleshoot the networking problem on IPv6 networks. The tools in this suite include tools from packet crafting tools to the most elaborate IPv6 tool out there for network scanning which is scan6 tool.

The following list will give you an idea of all the tools in the suite.

- addr6: A tool which analyzes an manipulates the IPv6 network

- flow6: And IPv6 security assessment tool

- frag6:A tool that performs fragmentation based attacks on an IPv6 network to perform a number of fragmentation related aspects and security assessment

- icmp6: A tool that performs attacks on the basis of errors thrown by ICMPv6 network protocol.

- jumbo6: A tool that looks at the handling of IPv6 jumbograms andassesses potential flaws in it.

- na6:A tool that sends arbitrary messages of neighbor advertisements.

- ni6: A tool that checks the potential flaws in processing ICMPv6 packages by sending information messages of the ICMPv6 node.
- s6: A tool that sends messages of arbitrary neighbor solicitation.
- ra6: A tool that sends messages of arbitrary router advertisements.
- rd6: A tool that sends messages of arbitrary ICMPv6 redirects.
- scan6: A tool that scans IPv6 networks

SlowHTTPTest

The SlowHTTPTest is a Kali Linux tool that can simulate the Denial of Service attacks in the application layer. It is supported on most platforms such as Linx, OS X and the command line interface on Windows systems.

The tool basically implements Dos attacks of application layer which are low bandwidth in nature such as Slow HTTP POST, slowloris, Slow Read attack by leeching the concurrent pools of connection, and also the Apache Range Header attack which causes high load on the CPU and memory of a server.

The HTTP protocol due to its design, to be completely processed, requires the request to be received by the server completely. This is what the slowloris and HTTP POST denial of service attacks take advantage of. The server will reserve its resources for pending data if the HTTP request is incomplete or the rate at which the data is transferring is very slow. Thus when the server is keeping most of its resources busy, it results in the creation of denial of service. That is exactly what this tool does. It sends partial or slow HTTP requests which keeps the server busy and thus resulting in a denial of service from the target HTTP server.

Maintaining Access Tools

Once we have cracked into a target machine by using the many methods that we have looked at, our next step should be ensuring techniques that will help us maintain the precious access that we have gained. This is to make sure that if the vulnerability that let you into the system gets patched in the future, you still have some way through which you can access the system.

We will look at the various tools available in Kali Linux, which will help us to maintain access to a system.

Cryptcat Package Description

CryptCat is a simple Kali Linux utility, which reads all data that it sees across network connections and writes data to it too. It uses the UDP or TCP protocol to do this and even encrypts the data that is sent over the network. It is designed in a way such that it can be integrated in a program or a script that runs in the front-end on a graphical interface while the tool runs in the backend in a very reliable manner. At the same time, it is also a tool, which is rich in features and allows network debugging and exploration. It is a very interesting tool as it will allow you to create the connection of your choice and has many other built-in features as well.

HTTPTunnel Package Description

The HTTPTunnel is a Kali Linux tunneling software. It can create tunnels through network connections. It basically has two components.

The client side which exists behind a firewall and will accept connections on ports that are connected to a remote server or will play the role of SOCKS proxy. The authentication source for SOCKS source can be a list of fixed users which is fetched from a MySQL or LDAP directory. The client component is aPerl script that is independent of platform or is also available as a Win32 binary.

The server side component exists on the Internet to which the client makes HTTP requests. The server side then translates and forwards these requests to network connections on upstream servers, which are remote.

There are two available servers. A web server, which basically hosts a PHP script. The PHP script that you host on the web server will allow your web server to act as the server to run HTTP tunnel.

The second server is a standalone server, which runs a Perl script independent of the platform or a Win32 binary. If you have your own box like a home computer, which is connected to the Internet, it can be used as the standalone server. Hosted server may pose restrictions to the PHP script (such as maximum execution time for the PHP script which will result in limiting the time for your connections) that you are hosting on it based on the company that is providing you the hosted server. Therefore, having a standalone server of your own has an advantage over the hosted server as you have complete access to your home computer.

Intersect Package Description

Intersect 2.5 is a Kali Linux tool that is the second major release in the version that have been released so far. There is a vast difference between this release and its previous versions. This version lets the user control which features are to be included in the intersect script and has also made room for importing customized features.

The latest release mostly focuses on the ability to integrate customized intersect scripts and also on the integration of individual modules and features in the tool. The user can use the create.py application which will guide him through a user friendly process which is menu-driven and lets the user add the modules of their choice, import custom modules and create intersect scripts as per their specific requirements.

Sniffing and Spoofing Tools

When it comes to network security, Sniffing and Spoofing of packets are two very important concepts as these are two of the major threats to the security of a network. If you want to deploy security measures for a network infrastructure, understanding the treats of packet sniffing and spoofing is very important. There are many tools available on the Internet, which facilitate sniffing and spoofing such as Tcpdump, Wireshark, Netwox, etc. The tools are used extensively by both attackers and security researchers. Students should also be able to use these tools. However, it is important to understand network security to be able to learn how to make use of these tools and how packet sniffing and spoofing is used in software.

Let's go through a few tools, which are used for packet sniffing and spoofing.

Burp Suite

Burp Suite is a Kali Linux tool, which serves as a platform to run security tests on web applications. It has a number of tools that work together and make the whole testing process work seamlessly right from the initial mapping of the test and analyzing the attack surface of the application, to finding the vulnerabilities in the security and exploiting them.

Burp lets a user have full control as it allows manual techniques to be combined with automation. This helps in making the whole process effective, fast and more fun.

DNSChef

DNSChef is a highly configurable Kali Linux tool for configuring DNS proxy for Malware analysts and Penetration Testers. A DNS proxy is a fake DNS is a tool that is used for analyzing network traffic.

For example, if someone is requesting for example.com over the Internet, a DNS proxy can be used to redirect them to an incorrect page over the Internet as opposed to the real server on which the website for example.com resides.

There are a lot of tools for DNS proxy available on the Internet. Most will allow you to point the incoming DNS queries to one single IP. DNSChef was developed a complete solution for a DNS proxy tool, which would provide a user with every kind of configuration that is needed. As a result of this vision, DNSChef is a tool that works across all platforms and is capable to create fake responses while supporting multiple types of DNS records

The use of a DNS proxy is advisable in times when you cannot force a web application to use a specific proxy server. For example, there are some mobile applications, which discard proxy settings in the OS HTTP settings. In cases like these, use of a tool like DNSChecf as a DNS proxy server will come handy. It will allow you to redirect the incoming HTTP request to a desired destination by tricking the application.

Wifi Honey

Wifi Honey is a Kali Linux tool, which is essentially a script that creates five monitor interfaces. One window is used for the tool airodump-ng and the remaining four are used for APs. The tool runs the five windows in a screen session making it simple to switch between the five screens and ultimately makes this process even more comfortable. All the sessions are labelled and therefore you will not end up getting confused with the screens.

Password Attack Tools

As the name suggests, password attack tools in Kali Linux help crack passwords of applications and devices.

Let us go through a few of the password cracking devices that are available in Kali Linux.

crowbar

Crowbar, which was previously known as Levye is a Kali Linux tool which is used for penetration testing. According to authors of regular brute forcing tools, crowbar was developed to brute force protocols in a manner, which was different than the regular tools. For example, during an SSH brute force attack, most tools use the username and the password to carry the attack but crowbar unlike the majority of the tools, uses SSH keys. This means that is there was any kind of a private key that was retrieved during any of the penetration tests, it could then be used to attack servers which have SSH access.

john

John the Ripper is Kali Linux tool, which is both fast and feature-rich in its design. You can customize it to your specific needs and it also combines many other cracking methods in one simple program. There is a built-in compiler, which is a part of the C compiler, which will even allow you to define a cracking mode which is completely custom. John is available on all platforms, which means you can use the same tool everywhere you go. Additionally, if you started cracking a session on one platform, you could very well continue it on another platform. Such is the portability of John.

John, out of the box, auto detects and supports the following crypt types in Unix by default.

DES based tripcodes, Windows and Kerberos/AFS hashes, OpenBSD Blowfish, FreeBSD MD5, BSDI extended DES, bigcrypt and traditional DES.

Ncrack

Ncrack is a Kali Linus tool, which is high speed and used to crack network authentication. The motive for building this tool was that corporates could check their network infrastructure and devices proactively for any flaws and loopholes such as poor passwords. Ncrack is also used by security professionals while conducting audits for their clients. A command line syntax similar to Nmap, a modular approach, and a dynamic engine that would take feedback from network and adapt its behavior, were the foundations that Ncrack was built up on. Nmap allows auditing of hosts on a large scale and that too in a reliable way.

Ncrack's list of features provide an interface that is very flexible and gives the user full control of the network operations, making it possible to perform brute force attacks that are very sophisticated in nature, providing time templates for easy usage, a runtime interaction that is much like Nmap's and many other things. Ncrack supports the protocols such as OWA, WinRM, MongoDB, Cassandra, MySQL, MSSQL, PostgreSQL, Redis, SIP, SMB, VNC, POP, IMAP, HTTP and HTTPS, Telnet, FTP, RDP and SSH

RainbowCrack

RainbowCrack is a general propose Kali Linux tool, which was an implementation of Philippe Oechslin. It is used to crack hashes, which have rainbow tables. Rainbow Crack cracks hashes of rainbow tables by making use of the time-memory tradeoff algorithm. This makes it different from hash crackers that are brute force.

A brute force hash cracker will generate all the plaintexts that are possible and then compute the hashes that correspond to the plaintext, all during runtime. It will then compare the hashes that need to be cracked with the hashes in hand. If no match is found even after comparing all available plaintexts, all results of the intermediate computation are discarded.

A time-memory tradeoff hash cracker sets up a stage for pre-computation, and all results of all hashes are stored in rainbow table. This is a time-consuming computation. But on the first stage of pre-computing is over, hashes that were stored in the rainbow table can be cracked with a performance that is much better and efficient as compared to a brute force cracker.

Chapter 5) Real World application for Kali Linux

If you feel that hacking is a skill that you are interested in and possibly you have gained experience yourself perhaps in less ethical methods, you may be interested in a career in hacking. As we mentioned earlier, many corporations and institutions often hire white hat hackers in order to improve their security capabilities and keep abreast of all developments in hacker culture.

There has never been a better time to be involved in the IT security field with the Bureau of Labor Statistics estimating that the sector is set to grow approximately 18 percent by 2024. Even more exciting for newcomers to the field is that the demand for skilled hackers is up by 40% according to a survey completed by the Ponemon Institute. This indicates that within the last few years there is roughly 40% of positions going unfulfilled within the IT security field. This could also be an indication that many skilled hackers are not willing to put their skills to use in a legitimate career, creating opportunities for white hat, ethical hackers.

As we mentioned earlier, there are many opportunities being created for ethical hackers to perform penetration tests to determine the viability of a networks security. For the right person, this type of work can be incredibly rewarding with pay exceeding six figures per year. The average security analyst in the United States makes over $96,000 per year.

As we rely increasing on technology and the constant developments in the IT field, the demand and job prospects for IT security professionals will continue to grow as the skills and requirements for hacker's change. An ethical hack is tasked with consulting an organization in how they are able to reduce the number of vulnerabilities that could be exploited by black hat hackers and working with developers to advise on how they are able to better address their security requirements. This leads to the updating of security policies and procedures and further training of staff as part of a company's security awareness and training program.

Job Requirements for Hackers

Despite the significant shortage and demand for ethical hackers, there are still requirements for an entry level ethical hacker to find himself a position within the IT security field. As a minimum, most white hat hackers will require a bachelor degree within computer science or a related field to secure an interview within an organization. Further from that the hacker will also require specific security certifications which will demonstrate that the hacker possess the appropriate level of experience and skill to perform the job to the best of their knowledge. Evidence for this has been demonstrated by the SANS Salary & Certification survey of 2008 in which 81% of respondents within the IT security field stated that having certifications was a key factor in securing their positions.

There are three primary security certifications which are recognised within the industry and although there is an abundance of other certifications, these have the greatest value when looking to secure a position.

Certified Ethical Hacker (CEH)

Before enrolling, students should at the very least have a basic understanding of Windows and Linux system administration as well as TCP/IP and virtualization. Classes are not compulsory, and students are able to enrol and opt to just take the exams provided they are able to submit proof that they have prior experience within IT security, 2 years to be exact.

The flexibility of the CEH certification is one of the most valued advantages of the course. Students are able to learn through self-study and video lectures which they are able to go through at their own pace and even the instructor led lessons are able to be taken online. If students are already employed with a business or organization in the security field, they are able to bridge their training in conjunction with their work.

The course is broken down over the course of five days, with each day being eight hours long. Students are able to access online labs for six months following their enrolment. As we mentioned earlier, the exam is comprised of 125 multiple choice questions over the course of four hours with a 70% minimum pass threshold to receive certification.

The general knowledge of the course provides students with an all-round experience of what is expected of them in the industry with no specific focus on any software, product, technology or skill. Students are expected to understand how to correctly scan a network to identify basic viruses as well as how to perform penetration testing and how a web server can be hijacked. Another element of the course is the social engineering aspect of hacking, informing hackers how they are able to manipulate and influence individuals to obtain personal and confidential information in order to infiltrate a computer system. In recent years, particularly as human communication has advanced to the point of online messaging and social media, social engineering has become a crucial element of hacking.

The course does have some drawbacks however being incredibly dependant on text and video instruction without too much of a focus on the hands-on practice. It has also been noted by industry experts that the course is somewhat outdated and is too simple for providing enough scope for day to day use. It does however present an excellent overview of the industry and those hackers looking to specialise are welcome to explore further certifications to gain more precise knowledge. The CEH is a more cost-effective certification to gain an insight into the industry and should not be treated as anything comprehensive.

The CEH certification is well known within the IT security field and having the qualification is a significant advantage to have documented on your resume. While it won't make you stand too far out from the crowd of other applicants, the certification will enable you to be on the radar of potential employers being the most recognised certification in the industry.

Network Penetration Tester (GPEN)

For those looking at expanding their skills in network penetration testing, the GPEN is the course to take you much deeper into this particular field of knowledge. The course takes students through what is involved in a penetration test before taking the GPEN test to obtain their certification.

Before undertaking a network penetration testing course, students should at the very least have an understanding the different types of cryptography within Windows, Linux and also an understanding of TCP/IP, many courses offer refreshers on these subjects to bring students up to speed but the prior knowledge will help when progressing through the course they are however not set in stone prerequisites.

Throughout the course, students will take part in over 30 labs, getting hands on practical experience through the pen-testing process with everything from detail reconnaissance, scanning and how to write and interpret a penetration testing report for conveying such information to management and technical staff. This will allow students to have a good idea of what is required when performing penetration tests in a corporate environment.

Coursework is generally completed through a Linux distribution containing everything the student will need such as Metasploit tools and free open source software such as password-breaker John the Ripper, taking advantage of some of the most widely used and most advanced tools the industry has to offer.

The course also aims to open students up to the perspective of the hacker when attacking the business, changing the mindset of students to approach the penetration in a way that they are able to think outside of the box and launch the attack in ways that would have been unintended from the point of view of the business.

The costs involved with the course can be a deterrent, particularly for those who are looking to break into the industry, however the practical hands on experience will allow students to present themselves as a cut above the rest and provide themselves with a career boost and a significant raise if they are currently working with the industry. The course can be difficult to get through with a huge amount of information presented over six days. The practical experience however will allow students to refine their skills as an ethical hacker and open new avenues in their career.

The exam consists of 115 multiple choice questions and is open book. The timeframe for the exam is run over three hours with students requiring a 74 percent pass threshold in order to receive the certification. The cost of the course varies whether you decide to take the online option or the in-person training with the latter being more considered once the compulsory online labs are taken into account.

Offensive Security Certified Professional (OSCP)

The OSCP is by far the most technical and specialised certification of the three. The certification is aimed towards providing an in depth and hands on insight into the penetration testing process and lifecycle. The certification aims to steer away from a classroom setting instead opting to be more focused on the practical aspects.

Students are first expected to complete the Penetration Testing with Kali Linux (PWK) course a course which has been built around the Kali Linux Distribution open source project which is maintained by the administers of the course, Offensive Security. Students will need to have a solid understanding of TCP/IP, networking and reasonable Linux skill as a minimum requirement.

The course is offered online with the only live training facility being in Las Vegas, Nevada. The cost of the course is determined by the length you will be accessing the online labs with options for 30 days and 90 days. During this time, you will be provided with video lessons, access to the labs and finally the certification test.

The OSCP is unique in that the test is not performed by multiple choice and instead is performed through a virtual networking in which you are tasked with researching the network, identifying vulnerabilities and then hacking the system to obtain administrative access similar to how a simulation would work. You are then asked to provide a comprehensive penetration test report to detail your findings, creating an environment that would mimic that of a real-world situation. The test is completed over 24 hours with the report being reviewed by a certification committee to obtain a passing grade.

While the OSCP is designed to develop skills focused on pen-testing tools and techniques, the certification also explores more out of the box thinking and unique approaches to solving problems. The test is structured in a way that students learn how to think laterally and that students will be able to not only find and exploit vulnerabilities but also further escalate their privileges and gain experience in scenarios that they may be faced with in the future.

The test is geared more towards advance security personnel in the IT field, with the hands-on approach taking much time with the trial and error approach however, this is incredibly beneficial for those looking to advance in the industry. Students are able to learn from hands on experience rather than just knowledge and are able to put their skills into practice in real scenarios.

There are downsides to the course however with students not being able to speak with a live instructor in the case that they may need to ask questions or may be stuck and require assistance in the labs. The course is also far less recognised than the CEH which can mean that you will not necessarily standout from the field of other applicants as well as you would with a more recognised course. The education however will provide you with a greater understanding of pen-testing, increasing your productivity and performance while at work which is something that cannot be said of other more knowledge based courses.

If a hacker wants to have an in depth understanding of pen-testing and become a specialist in their field, the OSCP will provide that level of experience and skill through the simulation exam, more so than any other course.

Which is the Best Course for You?

Your decision to take on any one of these courses will be founded in having a desire to further develop your knowledge and skills within the topics that are presented. Each one has its own pros and cons within the industry and it is down to the ethical hacker to decide where they are in their career and where they would like to take it. For example, for those who are looking to get started with a shift in their career and hoping to break into the industry, the CEH will provide them with the broad knowledge required and industry recognition for them to be considered for the position, however the information may be outdated and not for those who are looking to specialise or become exceptionally skilled in the industry.

If a student aims to develop their skills further and have a more comprehensive understanding of penetration testing, the GPEN uses tools that are widely used in the industry and allows for one on one instructions. The course also explores the social engineering aspect of hacking which is widely becoming recognised as a very important element of hacking particularly in the age of social media and technology dedicated to communicating, while still lacking high security measures. This can provide a career boost for one who is looking to increase their qualifications and their pay however the course comes at a cost.

Finally, if you are looking to specialise in pen-testing and have an understanding of the entire process the OSCP will provide you with extensive knowledge tested through a simulation scenario and while the course is not recognized as widely as the other courses, you can be sure that your practical experience in the workplace is of the highest standard. The lack of instruction and heavy course load can be overwhelming for beginners and therefore this course is recommended for those who have experience working within the IT security field as opposed to those who are looking to start in the industry.

Chapter 6) Wireless Hacking and penetration testing

The proliferation of readily available Wi-Fi networks has made Wi-Fi one of the most common network mediums. Wi-Fi is in many ways superior to traditional copper wire physically connected networks. Aside from the convenience of connectivity and the flexibility of network configurations that wireless networks afford the users, the lack of physical infrastructure needed to complete the network makes it much cheaper and easier to implement than Ethernet. With this convenience, however, comes certain security concerns that are not associated with traditional hardwired networks. With a copper or fiber-based network, a physical connection is needed for a new machine to join the network.

Wi-Fi Attacks

In order to conduct a Wi-Fi attack a hacker needs, at a minimum, a computer (normally a laptop) that can run scripts which are used to decipher the Wi-Fi password. They also must acquire a special Wi-Fi adapter that can be purchased relatively cheaply. A list of suitable Wi-Fi adapters can be found on hacker resource websites, but in general the adapter must have a feature known as "monitor mode" in order to be able to execute a Wi-Fi attack. It is important to note that not all Wi-Fi adapters that can be found at retail computer supply stores have this feature, and most internal laptop adapters are not appropriate. In general, hackers prefer to use some sort of Linux distribution, usually Kali, to conduct a Wi-Fi attack because most of the readily available tools were written for the Linux OS and come preinstalled on Kali. It is also possible with some configuration to run Linux on a virtual machine within another OS to mount a successful attack. Although attacks from other operating systems are possible, it is much easier for the beginner to conduct them from either a native Linux distribution or a virtual machine. A hacker-friendly distribution like Kali is recommended.

The detailed procedures and recommended programs for conducting Wi-Fi attacks against the various encryption protocols changes over time, although the general principles are the same. For the simplest attack, which is against WEP encryption, the general steps are as follows:

1)   monitor and view all Wi-Fi traffic in the range of the adapter while in "monitor mode" (set by a program called **airmon-ng**) using a program called **airodump-ng.**

2)   choose a target Wi-Fi network that is using WEP encryption and make a note of the name (ESSID) and network address (BSSID in the form XX:XX:XX:XX:XX:XX)

3)   restart **airodump-ng** to begin capturing network traffic from the specific network that you are targeting

4)   wait for a sufficient number of packets to be captured (this may take longer on networks with less traffic)

5)   use a program called **aircrack-ng** to piece together the captured network packets into a coherent password

WPA encryption cannot be cracked passively and requires the additional step of packet injection. Cracking WPA can take longer and is a more invasive procedure, but it is not much more difficult than cracking WEP. A program called **reaver**, normally available on the Kali distribution is typically used by hackers to crack WPA. WPA-2 hacking is a much more advanced concept for more experienced practitioners.

Penetration testing is a simulated attack on a computer system, network or server that analyses and assess vulnerabilities and weaknesses within the system security and once identified the hacker is able to gain access to the features on the system and steal the data.

The process is designed to identify a target system and is approached with a specific goal in mind. The test will then gather data and analyse the information presented to it and determine the most viable option to achieve the chosen objective.

There are two distinct targets which a penetration test will be directed towards. These are white box and black box. The white box target is one which provides a breakdown of the background and system information whereas the black box supplies nothing other than the company name. The main mission of the penetration test is to assess the weaknesses within the system's defences and vulnerabilities which could be exploited. The test will provide details of which areas of the system's defences have failed and supply this information as a means of improving these areas. This data is then sent back through to the system administration who will then use the reports compiled by the penetration test to determine a course of action and how the organization can implement countermeasures to avoid future attacks, exploiting these vulnerabilities.

The goal is largely dependent on the organization and their requirements for their system. The penetration test is also broken down into five phases which will also cover in greater detail for each phase. These phases are Reconnaissance, Scanning, Gaining Access, Maintaining Access and Covering Tracks. Penetration tests are available through a number of tools some of which are supplied operating systems as well as free software depending on the uses for each one, whether in a commercial or domestic sense.

Phases One: Reconnaissance

Before one undertakes a penetration test, they must first enter the reconnaissance phase or the discovery phase. This involves collecting preliminary data on the target in question and how it operates. This phase is generally the longest of the five and can take as long as a few weeks or even months. Data is collected by a number of means and the lengths that hacker goes to in order to obtain data will depend upon the backers own objectives and whether they are working in an ethical white hat sense or if their means of attack is that of a black hat.

The data collected can come through methods such as:

- **Internet searching**

- **Social Engineering Techniques**

- **Dumpster Diving**

- **Domain name management/search services**

- **Non-Intrusive network scanning**

For an organization to defend against a hacker in the reconnaissance phase they will need to go to great lengths as it can be quite difficult. This is because most organizations will have some degree of public presence or their information can be found across the internet in some form. As we mentioned before the method for obtaining data can be as simple as social engineering in which the hacker is able to coerce employees to provide information. This could even happen over a long period of time in which the hacker continuously sources small pieces of information from employees and overtime they are able to complete the puzzle and discover opportunities where there are security weaknesses and vulnerabilities that can be exploited.

This isn't to say there aren't things an organization can do to protect themselves from this type of hacking. For example, certain pieces of information can be kept confidential such as version numbers and patch levels of certain software, email addresses should be hidden from public view on websites as well as the names and positions of key personnel and where they stand in the overall company structure in relation to other members of staff.

Training can be undertaken to ensure staff members follow the correct protocol when dealing with confidential data such as destroying documents that have printed information rather than simply tossing it in the recycling or garage. They should also be warned when communicating with people they are unfamiliar with and avoid providing any information without proper clearance. This can be done through white hat methods, with hackers simulating an attack to ensure that employees are assessed in their handling of confidential information.

In terms of online information, contact information and domain name registration lookups should be generic and network devices should be protected from scanning attempts.

By taking these precautions, the organization can have a less likely chance that a hacker will be able to access the information required for an attack. This doesn't mean they won't attempt or continue to pressure the organization to gain access and there is still a chance that they can ultimately obtain access, it does however make the job much harder for them and have a higher probability of being caught.

Phase 2: Scanning

The hacker takes the information that has been collected during reconnaissance phase and from there assesses the data that has been compiled. From this, they are able to have an understanding of how the business operates and the value of the information that can be access during the attack.

Once the attack weighs up the value of the data that can be accessed from their assessment of data collected, they move through to the scanning phase. The scanning phase involves scanning the perimeter and internal network comprised of all devices and seeks to discover a weakness that can be exploited. There are ways in which scans can be detected such as through Intrusion Detection Solutions (IDS) or Intrusion Prevention Solutions (IPS) however these are not always effective as hackers are continually advancing and creating new circumnavigational techniques to avoid such controls. As hackers advance their techniques and tools, so too do the tools of security services, providing protection to the systems that are used by organizations. This is done through patches and releases of preventative solutions therefore it is best to consistently update software and security tools to ensure you have protection in the latest advances of black hat hackers.

There are some methods which system administrators can employ to ensure there is a reduced risk of an attack occurring or scans being performed on the system. For example, an administrator could shut down all ports that are no longer being used and close down any services that could be hijacked. Critical devices which are used for processing sensitive information should be set to only respond to devices which have been approved to avoid external devices taking advantage of their freedom of use.

Scanning is performed using a number of tools and applications on the behalf of the hacker. We will have a further look into the tools used in penetration testing further along in this chapter. Scanning is similar to the reconnaissance phase however it is at a more targeted level, scanning the target that is to be attacked whereas the reconnaissance phase is directed more towards the organization. Once the hacker has secured an even more defined target, the entry point, they are to move onto the next phase. Gaining Access.

Phase 3: Gaining Access

This the climax of the penetration attack. The hacker now has access to the resources available on the database of the organization. The hacker is then free to either extract the information that he sees of value or he is able to take control of the network and use it as a base to launch further attacks against other targeted networks in how we described a DoS attack. By gaining access to the network, the hacker now has control over one or more devices.

As was the case in the preventative measures of scanning, there are some precautions that administrators and security personnel are able to take to ensure that devices and services are more challenging to access by legitimate users such as black hat hackers. This can involve restricting access of users such who have no legitimate day to day requirement to be accessing the devices. Furthermore, security managers should be closely monitoring the domains and those who are accessing services such as local administrators. Using physical security controls will allow managers to detect attacks that are occurring in real time and can deny access while also alerting the proper authorities to ensure the intruder is exposed.

Another approach which can be taken to ensure that access is denied is to encrypt highly sensitive and confidential information using protection keys. This would mean that any attacker attempting to access the system regardless of how well the system is protected, will gain access only to find that the information is scrambled and with the keys protected, the attacker would have no reliable method for using the data that has been encrypted. Encryption is a good final line of defence for particularly valuable data however it cannot be relied upon entirely in itself. Even if the attacker was to access the system and discover that the data is encrypted, they can still wreak havoc on the network and even disable it, causing significant damage as a means of sabotage. Even more alarming, the attacker could have control over the system and use it for further crimes which could be traced back to the organization's network.

Once the attack has gained access to the system, they are still far from being in the clear. Access is for a limited time, the longer the hacker is operating from the system, the greater the chances of being caught. The hacker must then shift to the next phase, maintaining access to ensure they are able to collect as much data as possible.

Maintaining Access

The hacker is working against the clock at this point and they must ensure they are able to maintain access long enough to succeed in what they had set out to do whether this was to steal critical data and information or to launch a further attack from the encumbered server. The hacker has been able to avoid detection up until this point, however they are still at risk of being caught and the longer they have access to the system, the higher the risk they could be detected.

While you can make use of both IDS and IPS devices to detect hackers accessing the system, you can also detect when a hacker is departing from the system. This is known as an extrusion and there are a number of methods this can be done. The primary way you can identify your system has been in use from an unauthorised assailant is by detecting file transfers to external sites from internal devices. This indicates that data is being transferred from your server and being sent to external source and if this source is unfamiliar, it could indicate theft.

Another method is to detect any sessions which have begun between servers in the internal data centre and external networks that are not under your control. Assessing the traffic mix per time interval can also indicate that there is external access to the system that is not in line with the regular practices of the business.

Once the hacker has remained in control of the system for long enough to achieve all their objectives, they are then to move onto the next stage which is to both prevent themselves from being caught and exposed as well as establish a basis for re-entry should they need to return.

Phase 5: Covering Tracks

The final step for the hacker to take involves removing any evidence of their intrusion as well as establish controls which can be used at a later time should they need to re access the system. These controls will also need to be hidden and undetectable to avoid their removal. This is obviously the most difficult stage to detect a hacker as they are deliberately removing information that could alert security personnel.

It is still possible at this stage to detect an intruder, however it is likely that your system would have experienced a breach of security and a loss of data as a result of the attack. In this case, the best course of action is to perform a system mind assessment to discover any activity or processes that exist on the system that are not in line with the normal operation of the business. Once you have been alerted of an attacker, even if the hacker has long gone, security protocols should be upgraded to combat future attacks.

You may find it valuable to explore security solutions such as anti-malware, personal firewalls, host based IPS solutions and an improvement on security protocols and training of staff to be able to detect future events themselves and prevent further damage.

Conclusion

Upon reaching the end of the book, you should possess all the necessary knowledge to begin ethical hacking practices. This includes everything from the basics to advanced hacking techniques for you to try. You should definitely remember to try the exercises in this book- the detailed guides will give you a good idea of what you can do and need to do to break into various hardware and software programs.

The next step is to expand on your knowledge and learn what you are capable of! Computer software and hardware are always advancing, meaning that you will always have something new to learn. Now that you understand the basics, you can browse online, look for new information, and put your skills to the test to advance your hacking knowledge.

www.ingramcontent.com/pod-product-compliance
Lightning Source LLC
Chambersburg PA
CBHW071131050326
40690CB00008B/1416